What People Are Saying About
So You're Going Overseas

"Today we send our best and brightest on international assignments to help them become the next generation of executives. We are counting on them to run Dupont in the future and believe *So You're Going Overseas* will be an invaluable help."

Michael W. Soulier, Director Human Resources
DUPONT

"*So You're Going Overseas* is the single most comprehensive and concise source of information on international assignments that I have found. The authors' insightful and fresh perspectives on all phases of an expatriate assignment have been a continual source of advice and encouragement for me as an expatriate in Japan. Every company would be wise to make this standard reading!"

Jon Robison, Director of Marketing, Japan
IOMEGA

"*So You're Going Overseas* is a practical and easy guide for helping individuals think about the difficult decision of taking an international assignment. Given the importance of international business at Colgate-Palmolive, this book has great value for all of our employees."

Jill Conner, Director — People Development
COLGATE PALMOLIVE

"Going overseas is fun and exciting to a lot of people. However, part of the fun and excitement will turn into stress and failure without proper planning and preparation. I highly recommend Black and Gregersen's book to individuals who plan to relocate overseas as well as to organizations that plan to send their professionals abroad."

Takashi Wada, Manager — International Human Resources
UNIVERSAL STUDIOS

"*So You're Going Overseas* is great! It is organized around the important questions an assignee is likely to have. It delivers key information in an easy to assimilate fashion and offers practical advice in plain talk."

Sue Plaster, Director — Leadership, Mobility, and Succession Planning
HONEYWELL

"As the saying goes — always enter into things with your eyes wide open. This book is just the eye opener you need, for an honest perspective and for planning a major life changing event. A great find for those considering a move abroad."

Robyn Mingle, Director — Human Resources
BLACK & DECKER

"*So You're Going Overseas* is an excellent guide to understanding and managing the personal and professional opportunities and risks of an international assignment. From what you should know before you go to navigating the potential pitfalls of repatriation, this book offers sound advice, practical suggestions, and thought provoking examples to help you get the most out of going overseas."

Marion Shumway, Oraganizational Capability Consultant
AMOCO ENERGY INTERNATIONAL

"Historically, many US-based companies and managers divided the world into two 'markets' — domestic and international. As globalization becomes pervasive, proactive managers and prepared companies recognize the need for experience that comes from working outside 'the comfort zone,' across multiple cultures and diverse markets around the world. Black and Gregersen have written a book that prepares managers for that eventuality."

Richard D. Hanks, Senior Vice President — Lodging and Sales
MARRIOTT INTERNATIONAL

Workbooks to Accompany

So You're Going Overseas

The workbooks are interactive companions to the handbook. Each is targeted to the unique needs of the individual (employee, spouse, teenager, and young child). Together they guide each family member—and the family as a whole—to make the most of the international assignment.

✈ *So You're Going Overseas Employee Workbook*

✈ *So You're Going Overseas Spouse Workbook*

✈ *So You're Going Overseas Teenager Workbook*

✈ *So You're Going Overseas Kids Workbook*

Other Books by J. Stewart Black & Hal B. Gregersen

Global Explorers: The Next Generation of Leaders (with Allen Morrison)

Globalizing Human Resources Through International Assignments (with Linda Stroh and Mark Mendenhall)

Other Books by J. Stewart Black

The International Business Environment (with Anant Sundaram)

Management: The Global Challenge (with Lyman Porter)

So You're Going Overseas

A Handbook for Personal and Professional Success

J. Stewart Black, Ph.D

Hal B. Gregersen, Ph.D

Global Business Publishers

Manufactured at FRANKLIN COVEY PRINTING.

Cataloguing-in-Publication Data available through the Library of Congress.

ISBN 0-9663180-0-5

CONTENTS

ACKNOWLEDGMENTS

A number of people have made this project possible, and we would like to acknowledge their help and influence.

- Our families who both endured and thrived on living and working in foreign countries.

- Mark Mendenhall, Gary Oddou, and Allen Morrison who have been colleagues and friends for years.

- Rita Bennett who encouraged this project from the outset and provided thoughtful feedback on the content.

- A variety of executives who offered encouragement and advice, including Jean Broom, Sven Grasshoff, Noel Kreicker, Jill Conners, Robyn Mingle, Marion Shumway, Craig Christensen, Gordon Finch, Jim McCarthy, Alicia Whitaker, Alan Freeman, Margaret Alldredge, Mikell Rigg-McGuire, Takashi Wada, Rich Hanks, Jon Robison, Cris Collie, and many others.

- The thousands of expatriates and repatriates who have helped us capture the essence of their international assignment experience through invaluable insights, stories, and on-going research cooperation.

J. Stewart Black
San Diego, California

Hal B. Gregersen
Provo, Utah

CENTER FOR GLOBAL ASSIGNMENTS

THE AUTHORS

J. Stewart Black, Ph.D.

Dr. Black received his undergraduate degree in psychology and English from Brigham Young University, where he graduated with honors. He earned his master degree from the business school at Brigham Young University, where he graduated with distinction. After graduation, he held the position of managing director of a management consulting firm in Japan. Dr. Black returned to the U.S. and received his Ph.D. in Business Administration from the University of California, Irvine. He subsequently held faculty appointments at Dartmouth College and Thunderbird (The American Graduate School of International Management). He has authored over 30 articles on all aspects of international assignments. Currently, Dr. Black is the managing director of the Center for Global Assignments.

Hal B. Gregersen, Ph.D.

Dr. Gregersen is an associate professor of international strategy and leadership at the Marriott School of Management at Brigham Young University and has written dozens of articles on international business. He is also a senior partner in the Center for Global Assignments and consults with firms around the world on international assignment issues. Dr. Gregersen has taught at Dartmouth College, Pennsylvania State University, Helsinki School of Economics and Business Administration, Thunderbird, and completed a Fulbright Fellowship at the Turku School of Economics and Business Administration in Finland. Dr. Gregersen received an M.A. degree in organizational behavior from Brigham Young University and a Ph.D. degree in management from the University of California, Irvine.

FOREWORD

The seed for this book was sown about twenty years ago when each of us had our first experience living and working in a foreign country (Stewart in Japan and Hal in Finland). In both cases, the experience did not go well initially. We struggled with difficult languages and strange cultures. We wrestled with trying to understand and to be understood. By the end, however, we each came to know wonderful people, beautiful lands, and fascinating languages. Those insights changed how we viewed ourselves and the world.

Later, we both returned to these foreign countries on subsequent international assignments–only this time we had families. This opened our eyes even wider as to the potential pinnacles and pitfalls of going overseas. Around us we observed friends and associates also on assignment and noticed their great triumphs and occasionally sad tragedies.

These first-hand experiences motivated us to research in-depth what makes someone succeed personally and professionally in an international assignment. It has been a rewarding undertaking over the last fifteen years. During that time, we have written dozens of articles and a comprehensive book on the topic (*Globalizing Human Resources Through International Assignments*). We have also consulted with a wide variety of companies about what they can do to help their people succeed.

Then one day while helping a family prepare for an international assignment, it hit us: the key to success in an international assignment is the individual! Certainly companies can do many things that help people succeed, but in the end, whether individuals succeed or fail depends on how *they* approach, manage, and take responsibility for their assignment. And that's why we decided to write this book–to help the individual succeed.

We had several ambitions in writing this book. We wanted it to be:

•**Balanced**	We wanted the book to be realistic–neither too negative nor too positive. International assignments are challenging, but they can be rewarding both personally and professionally.
• **Comprehensive**	We wanted to cover the major issues expatriates face, from selection through repatriation.
• **Practical**	We wanted to provide a handbook offering down-to-earth advice. We wanted people to have something they could use.
• **Principled**	We didn't want the book to be too theoretical or just another long list of do's and don'ts. If we had fallen into the *theoretical trap*, then people couldn't apply the ideas to their lives. If we had fallen into the *checklist trap*, people could get stuck when they encounter things that are not on the lists.

So we set out to write a book that provided a realistic preview of the major aspects of international assignments and offered down-to-earth advice, yet helped people understand the underlying dynamics of international assignments. We hope we have succeeded in this ambition and wish you the best on your journey overseas!

Chapter One

So You're Going Overseas!

Introduction

The tidal wave of globalization is no longer coming; it's here! You have the chance to catch the wave, and an international assignment can be the perfect surfboard for turning this wave into the most thrilling ride of your life. But like surfing any giant wave, courage, timing, preparation, balance, and skill determine whether you ride the wave successfully, or crash and wipe out.

You might ask yourself why catching this wave of globalization is so important. The simple answer is because it is *inescapable*. The tidal wave of globalization has already engulfed entire industries. The commercial aircraft, semiconductor, and computer are just a few of the industries that have been swallowed up in the waters of globalization. For example, whether executives at Boeing want to or not, they must think and act on a global scale. With research and development costs for the new 777 airplane at over $5 billion, Boeing has no choice but to capture its return on that investment through global sales. No single national market is large enough to support the enormous development costs of the 777.

Your industry and company may not yet be affected, but don't count on that lasting. If you are not wet yet, you soon will be. Globalization has moved beyond fad and rhetoric to competitive reality. We can no longer look across the street or even within our own national borders and win the battle in the global marketplace. We must be knowledgeable of customers, competitors, markets, economies, governments, technology, workers, and partners the world over.

To compete in this global business environment, companies are sending more people on international assignments. Over the past five years, the vast majority of European, North American, and Asian multinationals have sent more people on international assignments than in the previous five. Over the next five years, a strong majority expect a continued increase, and only a small percentage predict a decrease.

The fundamental reason for this increased need for international assignments is to facilitate the global integration and coordination of firms' worldwide operations. Still, the specific objectives can vary. Some assignments are quite technical in nature. It might be a ten-month assignment to install a new computer system in a German subsidiary. Or it might be a two-year assignment to transfer a particular technology to a joint venture in China. Other assignments, however, are more strategic in nature. It might be a three-year assignment to turnaround an ailing unit in France, or launch a new manufacturing operation in Vietnam.

Whether an assignment is technical or strategic in nature, each has great personal and professional developmental potential. The assignment may help you develop better market knowledge, acquire greater understanding of key international competitors, increase your awareness of your firm's global operations, gain insights into technical developments in other countries, broaden your interpersonal skills, or generate ideas about new business opportunities. The developmental objectives may be explicit or implicit. Either way, international assignments are *unique* in their developmental potential and power.

So if you have been thinking about whether an international assignment would be a smart career move, keep reading. If you have been offered an international assignment, read the first two chapters before deciding to go. If you have already accepted an international assignment, make sure you finish chapters five and six before you get on the plane. If you are already on the plane, read through chapter seven before it lands. If you are currently on an international assignment, don't put this book down until you've read it cover to cover. If you've just completed an assignment, *read the book in reverse order*, starting with chapter eight on repatriation.

THE CHALLENGE AND OPPORTUNITY

Seriously, though, if you're reading this book, you've probably already thought about some of the issues we will cover. You may have already talked with some experienced people or heard stories about international assignments — both positive and negative. As you heard various and conflicting tales, you may have wondered what the truth really is. It is all true. We have known individuals who state categorically that it was the best personal and professional experience of their life. We have also known people for whom the international assignment was a very poor personal and professional move.

International assignments have the potential to be either the worst or best experience of your life. The international assignment is just the surfboard. How the ride goes is mostly up to YOU!

On the tidal wave of globalization, international assignments are inherently challenging surfboards to ride. For example, we knew a family who had a rather unpleasant experience while on an international assignment. (We'll call them the Joneses.) They came home early from the assignment because Fred Jones was not doing well at work and his family was miserable. The poor performance overseas and the early return hurt Fred's career. The stress and strain of living in a new and unfamiliar country added unfortunate pressure to a struggling marriage and family relations. Going into the decision to accept the assignment, Fred assumed that because he had been a success in New York, he would do fine in Hong Kong. As a consequence, Fred did not take advantage of preparation and training opportunities. Unfortunately, what leads to success in the U.S. is not necessarily what leads to success in Hong Kong. Fred's family's small town, rural background and their lack of excitement about the assignment did not make for a winning combination. The congestion and "hustle and bustle" of Hong Kong did not fit the family's more deliberate pace and preferences.

Fred and his family are not alone. A significant percentage of all individuals sent on international assignments fail. Failure, however, is not limited to early returns. It surfaces as marginal performance, poor adaptation (personal and professional), disrupted family stability, damage to local relationships with employees, government officials, joint venture partners, customers, and suppliers. Given that international assignees usually cost their company three times what they would cost in an equivalent position back in their home country, an unsatisfactory performance rating during an international assignment can seriously damage the assignee's career. Families also pay the price of unsuccessful assignments in terms of strained marriages, interrupted spouse careers, and destabilized children.

The challenges, unfortunately, don't stop with the completion of the assignment. Of those completing an international assignment, a majority find it difficult to fully utilize their international experience upon returning home, and 20% end up leaving their company within a year or two of repatriation. Without appropriate repatriation preparation, many managers do not receive promotions over the positions they held during the international assignment, and many take a parallel or lower position upon repatriation. Unless you take active responsibility for the management of your assignment and repatriation, you might end up feeling that you would have been better off if you had "remained at home." The following expatriate managers' quotes reflect these sentiments.

> I believe I would have moved much higher had I not gone overseas.
> –Expatriate after a three-year assignment

> [Being an expatriate] has hurt my overall career. . . . Many promises are made when employees accept overseas assignments regarding career paths, but few are kept.
> –Expatriate after a five-year assignment

However, *these problems do not need to happen*. The first step in avoiding unfortunate personal and career consequences is to make sure that the nature and timing of the assignment match you and your family. Not every assignment is right for you and you may not be right for every assignment—or now might just not be the right time. You are the best person to determine if the match is right, and you are the best person to drive the assignment's success. Our objective is to provide support for you in making the right decision and in creating the best outcome.

At the same time, we offer words of advice. Few things in life will offer you similar professional and personal growth opportunities. However, to ensure that an international assignment provides you with all the development opportunities possible, you will need to manage the process actively. No doubt there are many business and human resource managers in your company who want to help you and make this assignment a success. Take advantage of their support and proactively guide their assistance. But in the final analysis, keep in mind that it is your career, your family, your life, and your assignment.

This book covers the major issues you should consider in taking an international assignment. While we closely examine each issue in various chapters, we want to give you a brief overview up front.

Selection

As we mentioned, an international assignment is a challenge. It is generally a mistake to oversimplify the world and assume that if you have been successful at home, you will do fine abroad. Though it would probably simplify our lives if doing business well were the same the world over, the truth is that people think, behave, and conduct business quite differently from country to country.

Chapter two examines the issue of selection in great detail. It addresses why companies send people out of the country, whether international assignments are a good career move, what family considerations are important, and what characteristics affect cross-cultural adjustment.

Chapter two describes a questionnaire you can complete to get a good idea of the extent to which you may be suited for an international assignment. Chapter three examines the financial issues you should consider before accepting or embarking on a stint overseas, and chapter four addresses the logistical considerations in getting ready for the move.

Training

Many individuals do not take full advantage of the training opportunities available. In cases where training opportunities are absent, people typically fail to take sufficient time to prepare themselves for the assignment. Failure to educate yourself adequately can significantly hurt your performance at work as well as personal or family happiness while overseas. Even fewer people take advantage of training opportunities *after* arriving in the country, and most fail to keep up their learning and education efforts during the assignment. Keep in mind that *you don't know what you don't know.* So without some training and education, how can you learn what it is you need to know?

Chapters five and six explore why international assignments and cross-cultural adjustment are so challenging. Chapter five addresses, from a practical perspective, the nature of culture and why living and working in a foreign culture can be such a shock. Perhaps most important, chapter six takes a careful look at the various types of training available and their relative value. It also provides practical suggestions on how to prepare yourself before and after you arrive in the international assignment.

Adjustment and Support

After arrival, most people experience "culture shock" — the feelings of anxiety, disorientation, and frustration of adjusting to life in a foreign country. Culture shock is a normal and predictable response. It is impossible to inoculate yourself to avoid culture shock. Even if such an inoculation were possible, it's probably not advisable. Many of the most valuable lessons learned will come from the anxiety and frustration of trying to understand the country and its culture, and from reconciling your way of doing things with the business practices and lifestyle in the host country. Still, if the disorientation becomes too severe, it can lead to serious professional problems, such as missteps in negotiations, lost business opportunities, insulted clients, poor relationships with business partners, and equally serious personal problems, such as depression, divorce, substance abuse, and child abuse.

Chapter seven examines common adjustment problems, and what you can do to effectively master the stresses and strains of living and working in a foreign country and culture. Chapter seven also addresses the whole issue of performance evaluation and what you need to do to manage effectively the performance appraisal process during your international assignment.

Repatriation

Repatriation can be personally and professionally the most challenging aspect of an international assignment. Though you might not expect it, most people experience culture shock when coming home. In fact, a majority of people experience greater culture shock coming home than they did going overseas. Consider the following quotes.

Be mentally prepared for enormous change when coming home. Expect repatriation culture shock to surpass the culture shock you might have experienced when you went overseas.

> –Expatriate returning from a seven-year assignment in Indonesia

Coming back home was more difficult than going abroad because you expect changes when going overseas. It was real culture shock during repatriation. *I was an alien in my home country.* My own attitudes had changed so that it was difficult to understand my own old customs. Old friends had moved, had children, or just vanished. Others were interested in our experiences, but only sort of. They simply couldn't understand our experiences overseas or they just envied our way of life.

> –Expatriate spouse returning from a three-year assignment in Vietnam

Without proper planning and preparation, you may also find repatriation at work difficult. The following quote reflects some of these potential problems.

> Treat coming home as a "foreign assignment" and spend time getting the "lay of the land." Don't expect any special treatment—you're basically a "new hire." Look out for yourself. . . . After being home for nine months and after giving 33 years of my life to this company, I still have no office to work in—just a "bullpen" with a temporary assignment.
>
> –Expatriate returning from a one-year assignment in England

Why repatriation can be such a challenge and how to effectively manage it are the two key topics in chapter eight. Essentially, chapter eight helps you bring your international assignment to a successful conclusion—just as this executive did after returning to Ford Motor Company.

After coming home, I took a position that gave me the opportunity to use what I learned while working at Mazda (majority-owned by Ford) in Japan for the last three years. The new job is terrific. Overall, coming home has been easy, since I returned to an area which deals specifically with international activities. In my new group, it is critical to know how Mazda works, and I have that knowledge.

PURPOSE OF THIS BOOK

We were motivated to write this book because we personally have experienced the positives and negatives of international assignments. We have seen both terrific and tragic things happen to our friends and associates. Over the last decade we have conducted numerous surveys and academic research on all facets of international assignments. We have written many articles about international assignments. This book condenses that practical knowledge from research and experience in one place to help you succeed. International assignments are far too complicated for a short book like this to provide all the answers, but hopefully, we can steer you in the right direction.

Empowerment

With this general purpose in mind, let us talk about our first specific objective: *to empower you.* To get the personal and professional rewards that international assignments offer, you need an in-depth understanding of the entire process, including the strategic role of international assignments, the process of cross-cultural adjustment, the dynamics of effective training, and the challenges of successful repatriation. While we will talk separately about the various aspects of international assignments, they are all interrelated and need to be understood collectively.

To be truly empowered, you need to conduct a deep and honest assessment of yourself. An international assignment is not for everyone; a particular assignment may be right for you, while another might not be; and now may or may not be the right time. If you decide to accept an international assignment, this book will help you take a careful look at how well you match the assignment, and how well it matches you. Rarely will the assignment and the individual be a perfect match. Most of us have weaknesses that will make the assignment even more challenging. But these same weaknesses can also enhance the developmental potential of the assignment. This book is designed to help you prepare adequately and remain watchful of problem areas so they don't unexpectedly reach up and bite you.

While we will answer many questions about international assignments, we cannot address every question. Still, the general questions we tackle should help you formulate the specific questions you need to ask in your particular situation. Many times, having the right questions is more valuable than having a long list of answers.

Preparation

A key to getting the right questions and answers is preparation. "Forewarned is forearmed." This saying may be trite, but it is also true. Consequently, we provide you with the four necessary ingredients of successful preparation.

1. **Areas of Preparation**. The first necessary ingredient for success is an understanding of the areas of preparation. We do this at both a general and specific level. We examine all the major areas, including selection, compensation, logistics, training, adjustment,

performance evaluation, and repatriation. We also examine a good number of specifics (that may or may not apply in your particular case). We hope that at the very least we will help you more clearly recognize those particulars so you can address them *before* rather than after the fact.

2. **Dynamics Of International Assignments.** The second necessary ingredient is an understanding of the dynamics to prepare for. If you understand the basic dynamics of cross-cultural adjustment, culture shock, or repatriation adjustment, you can "back into" preparation and specific questions or problems that might be unique to you. Without an understanding of the underlying dynamics, you would be left to simply follow the "ten easy steps to preparing for a move overseas" and be forced to discover later that three of the ten steps didn't really apply in your specific case, and two other steps that weren't listed were critical. To be adequately prepared, you must understand the basic dynamics of living and working abroad.

3. **Preparation Strategies**. The third necessary ingredient is understanding effective preparation strategies. We talk about a range of preparation strategies and what they can and can't do. Most people find that a well-rounded preparation requires a portfolio of approaches — no single method on its own is sufficient. We not only look at some general strategies and approaches that work for most people, we also explain why they work.

4. **Available Resources**. The fourth and final necessary ingredient is a knowledge of the various resources available to help you prepare. To keep this book short, we could not include all the possible information you

might need or want. As a compromise, in various sections we provide information on resources–including the accompanying workbooks–that you can go to for further information and detail.

Success

In the final analysis, our objective is the same as yours. We want your international assignment to be a personal, family, and career success!

International Assignment Cycle of Success

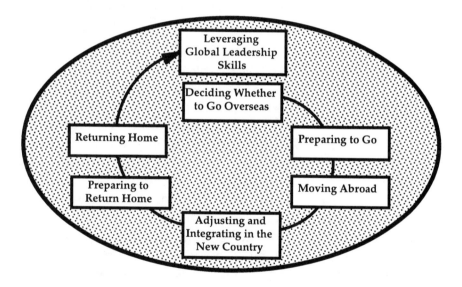

In talking with hundreds of individuals and families who have lived and worked overseas, we have been surprised by the convergence on what personal, family, and career success means. If you are like most people we've met and known, your personal objectives likely include the desire to grow and develop, to learn new things, and to improve your ability to relate to and work with people whose backgrounds are different from your own. If you have a family, you no doubt want the experience to bring your family closer together and help family members grow individually and benefit from the experience. On a career level, you no doubt want to gain knowledge and capabilities that allow you to add significant value in the future—value that will be recognized and rewarded by your company.

We believe that success in these areas is facilitated by both an understanding of the principles and dynamics involved, and a knowledge of practical recommendations. *In short, we provide you a practical but principled guide.*

The impact we hope the book will have is probably best reflected in a simple experience one of the authors, Stewart Black, had in preparing a couple for an assignment to Japan while he was a professor at Dartmouth. At the beginning of the predeparture training program, Stewart commented to the couple, "So you're going overseas." The husband and wife looked at each other, exchanging glances of terror, and the wife said, "Yes, and we're scared to death." On the last day of the week-long program, the couple and Stewart were eating in one of the school's dining facilities when another professor walked by. After introductions and a brief explanation of why the couple was on campus, the other professor commented, "So you're going overseas." The husband and wife again looked at each other, and then the wife said, "Yes, and we're excited and ready to go." If an international assignment is right for you at this point in time, and we can help with that assessment and preparation, then we will have done our job in helping you make your international assignment a personal and professional success.

Chapter Two

To Go
Or Not To Go?

To go or not to go on an international assignment is the fundamental question that only you can answer. As you prepare to make that decision, experienced international assignees suggest several factors you should consider:

- Why companies send people on international assignments

- How the assignment can impact your career

- Whether your family situation fits the unique challenges of an international assignment

- What key personal characteristics you need in order to succeed when working and living in another country

In general, an international assignment can be a great personal and professional experience, but not every set of personal circumstances match up with every international assignment opportunity or timing. In this chapter we address these issues so you can decide whether this is the right assignment and whether now is the right time.

WHY COMPANIES SEND PEOPLE ON INTERNATIONAL ASSIGNMENTS

If you look at why companies send people on international assignments, you will find many reasons— most are good, but some are not so great. On the positive side, companies often send people on international assignments to accomplish important strategic objectives, such as developing employees' global skills, coordinating and controlling key international operations, and transferring innovations throughout the worldwide organization. Sometimes the objectives are more tactical in nature, such as sending someone simply to put out a fire or solve an immediate problem, with no real thought about how the assignment fits into the person's future. When approached strategically, international assignments can benefit both you and the organization. When approached from just a tactical perspective, some "firefighters" end up feeling burned, not because anyone deliberately set out to burn them, but because international movements are complicated and require long-range planning to ensure that expected benefits actually occur.

As more and more companies see the pot of gold at the end of the globalization rainbow, they send more and more people on international assignments in search of that gold. To get a slight glimpse of the magnitude of people working overseas, consider that around 250,000 U.S. expatriates embark on international assignments each year. Over the past decade our research has consistently shown that most companies intend to increase even further the total number of expatriates. In order to ride the tidal wave of globalization, companies must have people with international savvy and experience who can recognize and capture international business opportunities.

TACTICAL ASSIGNMENTS OF THE PAST

In the past, international assignments were often designed with one objective in mind: put out the overseas fire! The fire in a foreign country might have been unusually high defect rates, questionable accounting practices, or disruptive labor relations. As a result, companies would choose people, give them a firefighter's hat, and send them to the rescue in a foreign location. For a moment, consider the following example of how tactical, fire-fighting assignments can easily (and quite unintentionally) turn into a recipe for failure.

Assignment: Sweden

Sue Harris, director of Emanon's environmental systems division, was on the phone with Bill Webster, her boss. Sue told him, "Only three and a half weeks before I have to send *somebody* to Sweden . . . but who?" Bill responded curtly from corporate headquarters in New York City, "*You* know your people better than I do, Sue. Just get somebody over there fast, and get things back on schedule!"

During the previous year, Emanon's Stockholm subsidiary, which was primarily responsible for product engineering, had missed several critical deadlines to complete the redesign of a market-leading pollution-control system. These delays had been costly, since the redesign was essential to Emanon's globally integrated production processes. Corporate headquarters wanted an immediate management change in Stockholm to ensure that the current redesign would be finished within three months,

---

and to set the Stockholm subsidiary on a straight course so that future engineering projects would stay ahead of production needs.

After talking with Bill, Sue spent the rest of the morning reflecting on who had the right technical background to manage the design process. After mentally reviewing the best qualified engineers in her division, Sue came up with a short list of three good candidates for the Stockholm job.

As Sue looked over the list, her mind turned again and again to Max Eisenhardt, one of the best engineers she had in the United States. Perhaps more important, he also fully understood the pollution-control systems being redesigned in Stockholm. Besides that, Max was a no-nonsense manager who had done a terrific job in fixing a product-engineering problem in the New Jersey plant over the previous three years. Without any more deliberation, Sue decided that Max was the right choice and set up an interview.

Two days later, Max flew from New Jersey to Sue's office in Chicago. During the interview, Sue explained that the Sweden job would not be easy. The Stockholm subsidiary had consistently missed deadlines on product designs, and its new manager must turn around the situation. Max responded with full confidence: "If I did it in New Jersey, I can do it just as well in Stockholm." Sue reminded Max that the opportunity carried high visibility in the firm, since corporate headquarters knew of the problems in Stockholm, and implied that whoever turned the operation around could expect a hero's welcome upon returning home. Max could see this international assignment as the ultimate career move: high challenge and high visibility. He couldn't wait to fly home to New Jersey and convince his wife and family that the Stockholm job was a once-in-a-lifetime opportunity.

Emanon's response to the staffing problem in Sweden reflects the way in which many U.S. multinationals approach the selection process for international assignments and how this approach can lead to unintended consequences. Basically, a crisis boiled to the surface in a foreign operation, and Sue had little time to assess the situation strategically or systematically. Her rush to put out the foreign "fire" resulted in focusing on candidates with the right technical qualifications to solve the current crisis. With little time to choose, Sue ignored the human resource department resources, and chose from a narrow range of candidates — the people she knew. She ignored the candidates' (and families') cross-cultural capabilities. As a result, Max was the right person for the wrong place and time. He had the best technical skills to build pollution-control systems, but the worst communication and management skills to build them in another country — Sweden. After two months in the position, the project fell even further behind because Max managed in Sweden the same way he had in New Jersey. The results? The project failed, Max returned from the assignment prematurely, and Sue's "poor choice" in such a high-profile situation stuck with her for years at Emanon.

Failures like Max's usually result when rapid-fire selection decisions put technically qualified people into overseas positions, positions that require far more than technical competence. In fact, most international assignment failures (either poor performance or premature return) result from ineffective cross-cultural adjustment, *not* technical incompetence. Nevertheless, firms too often rely solely on technical, job-related skills when selecting expatriates.

STRATEGIC APPROACH TO INTERNATIONAL ASSIGNMENTS

To ensure success overseas, one of the first things you need to do is approach the assignment strategically. This approach requires that you and your company consider three potential strategic objectives: developing employees; coordinating and controlling operations around the globe; and fostering worldwide innovation, technology, and information exchange.

Employee Development

CEOs around the world deeply care about developing employees with global perspectives and skills. Global companies need hundreds and sometimes thousands of employees who understand the unique needs of foreign customers, suppliers, employees, government policies, technologies, and so forth. To meet these needs companies require managers and employees who can work with people from different cultural, religious, and ethnic backgrounds. To foster these global perspectives and skills, international assignments provide invaluable training so you can play a pivotal role in your company's future global success.

Coordination and Control

Your international assignment might play a strategic role in the coordination and control of your company's global operations. Coordinating and controlling companies with facilities around the world can be a daunting challenge. Consider Phillips, headquartered in the Netherlands. It operates in over sixty countries on every continent of the world, with subsidiaries, joint ventures, and alliances from Austria to South Africa, from New York to New Zealand. Coordinating and controlling this sprawling company toward a common strategic objective, given the enormous geographical distances, cultural diversity, and conflicting government and customer demands is a big challenge. Policy manuals as control mechanisms in large multinational companies are of little use in coordinating and controlling activities because they can't cover all the different contingencies that arise as regulations, customs, cultures, and business practices change from country to country. Instead, it takes key people placed in strategic positions throughout the world. These people understand the global strategy and integration needs of the corporation, and at the same time make appropriate local adjustments to successfully implement their company's global strategy.

Innovation and Technology Transfer

During an international assignment, you may end up playing a pivotal role in locating and disseminating innovations and new technologies throughout your company. For example, if a firm intends to make several key strategic acquisitions throughout the world, it might need to move technology and information from operation to operation or from overseas subsidiaries to headquarters. People are the most effective transmitters of this information. For example, Toyota knows that sending people to Japan for three to five years is the only way it can transfer a proprietary approach to automobile production into other plants around the world. Through an international assignment, you can build a network of connections throughout your company to continue gathering and sharing new ideas with colleagues close and far away — even after the assignment ends.

Consider for a moment how strategic objectives *might* have played a key role at the Emanon Company, described earlier in this chapter. Specifically, Max Eisenhardt's assignment to Stockholm *might* have accomplished the transfer of key technologies. Max might have successfully transferred technology to the Stockholm subsidiary, as well as discovered new ideas that could be of benefit to other Emanon subsidiaries. But to make this transfer happen, Max needed better cross-cultural communication and management skills. Maybe Max could have become the right person with rigorous cross-cultural training *before* taking the assignment, or maybe Max was the simply the wrong person for Sweden — period. The point is that neither Max nor his company put themselves in a position to make this assessment, because both took a tactical rather than strategic approach to the decision.

CAREER CONSIDERATIONS

When offered an international assignment, everyone undoubtedly asks themselves: "Will an international assignment help or hurt my career?" We have asked this question of thousands of managers who were considering an assignment, were on assignment, or had returned from an assignment. Almost always the response is the same: "It depends." Among other things, the answer depends on how globalized your company is today and where it will be in the next five to ten years. It also depends on where *you* are today and where *you* want your career to be in the near and long-term future.

Company Globalization Plans

How globalized your company currently is makes a big difference in the immediate and long-term career benefits you can reasonably expect from an international assignment. Let's look at four profiles of company globalization to see how they impact the relative value of international experience. One qualifier first: just because an international assignment may not have an immediate career payoff does not mean the assignment should be turned down. As we will examine later in this chapter, personal, family, and other benefits may more than compensate for low career payoff. With that said, let's look at level of company globalization and career benefits of an international assignment.

For some companies, international activity consists primarily of *exporting*. Many of these companies simply export excess inventory to international markets. These international sales are viewed as nice additions to total company revenues, but they are usually not seen as strategic. At the export level, only a few people are required to make globalization work. These people are technical specialists, skilled at handling the quirky demands of exporting (such as foreign currency exchange, international letters of credit, custom regulations, and so on). Unless the company plans to move beyond exports, international assignments are not usually an essential step to the executive suite.

If international sales are large enough, companies often set up an *international division* to focus on international activities. At this level of globalization, companies set production targets with specific foreign sales in mind, though they typically fill domestic orders before international ones. Many of these companies take a "financial portfolio" approach and view international sales primarily as counterweights to domestic market cyclicality. For these companies, the total number of people involved in international activities is greater than in export firms, but it is still a relatively small number. For companies at this level, an international assignment may not be a requirement for senior managers, and taking such an assignment may not lead to immediate career payoffs. But if the firm is headed for greater globalization in the future, an international assignment can be a wise career move.

As international sales approach 25% of total revenues, most firms establish foreign subsidiaries in countries throughout the world. If these foreign subsidiaries operate independently, this is typically referred to as a *multidomestic* level of globalization—that is, the firm has multiple domestic operations in various foreign countries. Multidomestic companies typically support several small— but complete—in-country subsidiary organizations. In these corporations, a handful of managers are often sent on international assignments to ensure the proper operation of important foreign subsidiaries. However, most senior managers in these companies do not have international experience, and as a consequence, international assignments may not have huge, immediate career payoffs. However, we can cite dozens of companies that had this profile and then quickly wanted to move to a higher level of global integration but couldn't, because they lacked internationally savvy managers. So depending on where your company is going, an international assignment at this stage may have a medium-term career payoff.

When companies approach 50% international sales, *global integration* pressures often follow. International operations typically serve strategic versus opportunistic purposes. For example, they might serve as a blocking strategy: Kodak competes in Japan not because it expects to make a lot of money there (and it doesn't), but because Fuji—its main competitor—uses excess profits from its lucrative Japanese market to compete more successfully against Kodak in the U.S. Consequently, Kodak must compete in Japan, if for no other reason than to keep Fuji's Japanese profits down. Another strategic purpose is to amortize significant fixed investment costs over a greater revenue base, resulting in lower unit costs. For example, Microsoft sold Windows95™ around the world because it needed a massive worldwide revenue base to cover the software's enormous development costs of over one billion U.S. dollars. Most important, highly globalized companies like Shell, 3M, Ford, Colgate-Palmolive, or Nokia require a large number of managers and employees who understand the strategic role of international operations, who work effectively in other cultures, and who successfully lead multicultural teams. At this stage of globalization, internationally competent people add significant value to the company, and they can count on moving into positions of senior responsibility *only* after completing a successful international assignment.

As a general rule-of-thumb, the more globalized your company becomes, the more likely the career payoff of an international assignment in the short-term. At the export, international division, or multidomestic levels of globalization, it is often difficult to see an immediate payoff for international assignments. This does not mean that there are not career payoffs or that you should turn down an assignment; it just means that you should not expect career benefits to appear automatically on their own. However, when a company has integrated operations throughout the world, the terrain shifts significantly.

Employees with international experience, excellent technical skills, and superb cross-cultural savvy are usually in high demand and command a premium price.

Since it takes time for you to acquire international expertise and for your company to move to a high level of globalization, you need to make sure that you acquire international experience and skills well *before* your company needs them. This means you need to be able to *see the globalization future for your company* before it actually happens.

When considering an international assignment, ask yourself these key questions: What level of globalization is my company at today? Where is it going in the next five to ten years? What experiences do I need to prepare for those globalization activities? Your answers to questions like these will help you decide from a strategic perspective the nature and timing of a beneficial international assignment.

Personal Career Ambitions

In addition to a strategic career assessment, you need to make a *personal* career assessment. This involves a careful, accurate assessment of where *you* want to be in the future. For example, do you have ambitions to become a senior executive? If so, and your company is headed toward high levels of globalization, an international assignment is a required stamp on your senior executive passport. For example, Jack Welch at GE has told his managers,

> The Jack Welch of the future cannot be like me. I spent my entire career in the U.S. The next head of General Electric will be somebody who spent time in Bombay, in Hong Kong, in Buenos Aires. We have to send our best and brightest overseas and make sure they have the training that will allow them to

be the global leaders who will make GE flourish in the future.

We have heard comments like Jack Welch's from dozens of CEOs in highly globalized companies. But maybe your career ambitions lean less toward general management and more toward a functional area. If this is the case, before taking the assignment, carefully consider how an assignment can help you add value in a functional specialty such as marketing or engineering.

ASSIGNMENT CONSIDERATIONS

When considering an international assignment, you should know two important dimensions of the job: expectations and freedom.

Assignment Expectations

When working overseas, many different people hold expectations about an expatriate's performance. For example, your boss and the human resource department back home will have certain expectations about your performance during an international assignment. Sometimes these expectations are in sync with those held by local managers and employees, and sometimes they are in conflict. You may even have three major locales of expectations—corporate, regional, and local. Our research with expatriates has found that conflicting expectations are one of the most powerful factors in poor expatriate performance. Expatriates often unwittingly do poorly because they are unaware of different expectations, or because they get overloaded or overcompromise trying to placate conflicting expectations.

When deciding to take an assignment, you should be careful to understand the specific performance expectations that will be leveled against you from many different parts of the company. Think of yourself doing a 360° assessment of expected performance before you ever step into the job. People you may want to get a read on include a home country manager, a host country manager, and a human resources department representative. Write down the expectations others have of you if you were to take the assignment. These expectations should make clear the immediate purposes of the assignment (in other words, what fire should you put out?), and the long term intents of the assignment (specifically, employee development, coordination and control of operations around the world, and innovation transfers), and the extent to which incompatible expectations exist or not.

Freedom

Our research has also found that one of the powerful factors contributing to high performance in international assignments is freedom (sometimes called *job discretion* or *autonomy* by academic types). One successful expatriate explained the power of freedom in this way:

> Imagine that you are being pulled in three different directions at once and the path you can walk is only a foot wide. You have to choose one direction over the others, and someone is going to be disappointed. Now imagine the same thing [multiple expectations] but you have a path as broad as a field to walk. Now you may be able to creatively meet everyone's expectations.

As this illustrates, different or even conflicting performance expectations do not necessarily mean you should turn down the assignment, as long as it gives you enough freedom. On the other hand, you should seriously consider passing on or renegotiating the nature of an assignment that has incompatible expectations and little freedom.

FAMILY CONSIDERATIONS

The number-one reason for failed international assignments is spouse/family cross-cultural adjustment difficulties. If you are married and/or will be taking children with you, make sure that other family members are (1) motivated to go, and (2) capable of handling the assignment—the culture, living conditions, education system, and so on.

Spouse Considerations

However strong or weak your relationship and your communication patterns with your spouse, you need to put everything you have into really understanding your spouse's true feelings about an international assignment opportunity. You must listen as well as or better than you ever have before. We have encountered far too many couples who lament, "We wished we had talked about this more honestly and more in-depth." So take the time to really listen to your spouse's positive and negative views on the assignment. In the companion workbook, we provide a number of questions that may be helpful in starting and facilitating this type of discussion.

Spouse career ambitions are likely at the top of the list of topics that need extensive discussion. Given that over half of all married professionals have spouses who work, most couples will need to tackle this consideration. Although most companies do what they can to facilitate spouses working during international assignments, ultimately this is determined by the host government. Many governments restrict spouses from working. Consequently, this is a key issue that you will want to gather information on and discuss.

Still, even if the host country will not provide work permits for both partners, other benefits of the assignment may be worthwhile to your spouse. Our interviews and surveys of dual-career couples found that a variety of other benefits compensated for the career interruption and loss of income that an international assignment can cause. Often spouses used the time to pursue further education, including the completion of graduate degrees. Others found great rewards and personal development through volunteer activities. Simply put, many spouses enjoyed the break in their careers and saw the international assignment as a relaxing "time out." The point of these alternatives is not to convince you that any dual-career problem can be solved, but just to say that many dual-career couples have found solutions. For example, in one study we found that over half of all U.S. expatriates' spouses worked before taking international assignments, but fewer than 25% of these spouses worked during the assignment. Still, there was no significant difference in adjustment to or satisfaction with the assignment between single-career and dual-career couples.

In addition to in-depth conversations, a "look-see" trip can be very valuable in helping assess spouse considerations. The key to extracting the value of a look-see visit is arranging it as early in the decision-making process as possible and going into it with an open mind. If you wait to take the look-see visit until late in the decision-making process, it can easily become a "look and convince" visit because so much momentum has been built up. But even if you take the trip early in the process, it is critical that both you and your spouse go into it with open minds — *not blank minds, but open minds.* By this we mean that you should have a hundred questions that you hope to address during the visit, but you should try to hold off on the answers until you've seen things for yourself.

Children Considerations

If you will have children living with you while overseas, you are in the majority. In our research, nearly 70% of all expatriates have children with them during their assignments. Perhaps the biggest issue for children is education. Will the children attend local schools or international schools? What is the quality of both? Will the children have to learn the local language in order to attend local schools? How difficult will that be? Do the local or international schools have sufficient resources to meet any special learning or development needs of your children? Parents struggle with these and other important education questions. Checking out the educational alternatives in the host country is a critical activity, which you should definitely include in your look-see visit agenda. In general, however, research suggests that children of expatriates do as well or better academically than their counterparts who remain in the U.S. public school system.

In addition to educational issues, the challenges for children who leave home and have to develop new friendships during international assignments are often great. Research has found that children under the age of thirteen have the easiest time, while teenagers have the most difficulty. This does not mean that teenagers are doomed to have a terrible experience overseas. Quite the contrary, it can be a great experience for personal growth and maturity. It does, however, mean that greater communication and understanding will be needed if the positive benefits of living in a foreign country are to be captured for teenagers.

Other Family Considerations

Finally, you may need to consider other family issues, such as elderly care or minor children not living with you. Despite conversation, interviews, and surveys of literally thousands of expatriates, we have no hard-and-fast advice to pass along on these topics. All we can say is that in most cases, taking parents who have health problems with you to a foreign country with different medical standards or practices in the context of a foreign language can be a frightening proposition for everyone.

On the positive side, while an international assignment can make it more costly and difficult to visit with or keep in touch with minor children not living with you, arranging for them to visit you in the foreign country can be a tremendously positive experience for the children, especially if they visit you after you have been there long enough to learn the lay of the land, so to speak. You can use the visit to introduce them to a variety of cultural, historic, recreational, and educational activities and opportunities.

COUNTRY OF ASSIGNMENT CONSIDERATIONS

Without question, the specific country of assignment is important to consider. However, be careful not to come quickly to common and stereotypical judgments, such as "Paris would be lovely" or "I could never live in China." The fact that some countries or cities are generally more or less desirable does not mean that they hold the same allure or drawbacks for you and your specific situation.

Cultural Differences

Some countries no doubt have cultures that are easier to understand and adjust to than others. Later in chapter five we discuss in detail why this is so, but from a personal growth perspective, cultural difference is a dual-edged sword. On the one edge, the greater the cultural differences, the greater the adjustment challenges. It will likely be more difficult to understand the motives and behaviors of others and to feel like you fit in. It is likely to be more frustrating and challenging. On the other edge, the greater the cultural difference, the greater and potentially the more exciting the knowledge and experience acquired can be. The key is to be excited about and committed to growing and stretching. It means making sure that you take the time and put forth the energy to travel in the country, learn the language, take cultural classes, and get involved in activities during the assignment.

Living Conditions

When looking at a potential foreign assignment, it is important to focus on living conditions rather than living conveniences. Too often, expatriates who contemplate living in a particular country focus on what things would be convenient or inconvenient. For example, refrigerators in Japan and France are usually quite a bit smaller than in the U.S. This means more—and possibly daily—visits to the grocery store, and perhaps visits to separate vegetable, meat, and bakery stores. If you are looking at an international assignment and focus on all the inconveniences that will require change in your routines, you are focusing on the wrong things. An international assignment by its nature is about change. The key in assessing living conditions is not inconveniences, but health and personal safety. Daily walks to the various stores for food may be an inconvenience, but the exercise may also actually be good for your health. So many things about living in Japan may be more inconvenient, but the living conditions in terms of health and safety are quite high. While Japan is just an example, the point is that when assessing the country of assignment, it is important to focus not on living conveniences, but on *living conditions*.

Language

The ability to communicate is crucial to expatriates' success in global assignments. Most strategic functions of global assignments require individuals to communicate effectively in other cultures. Without some level of host-country language proficiency, it is very difficult to communicate genuinely with host-country nationals in a new culture. All things being equal, language proficiency is a tremendous advantage in trying to operate in a foreign land. As one expatriate explained, "The 'key' to understanding the host country is the language." The language is how host country nationals formulate and express thoughts and emotions. Even if you don't expect to become fluent in the language, take time to evaluate how easy or difficult some mastery of the language will be and what resources will be available to you in this pursuit.

PERSONAL CONSIDERATIONS

Fundamentally, you need to ask yourself two main questions relative to personal considerations: (1) What do I personally want to get out of this experience? and (2) Do I have the disposition and skills to be successful in this particular country and assignment?

Personal Objectives

As we mentioned earlier, even if you expect no immediate career payoff, you still may take the assignment for personal development reasons. Maybe you've always wanted to travel overseas, master another language, or broaden your understanding of a different culture or religion even if it didn't translate directly into enhanced career opportunities. An international assignment can represent unique personal growth opportunities that are worth pursuing. Our only caution is that we have seen a number of people take on international assignments primarily for personal development reasons, accomplish those personal objectives, and then expect others in the company to recognize and value those developments (through promotions or whatever). If you take an international assignment primarily for personal reasons, don't expect anyone else to reward you for accomplishing your objectives. They may, and personal accomplishments may translate into professional ones, but don't expect them to. Instead, if you take on an international assignment for personal growth, be happy within yourself for the development you achieve.

Personal Capabilities

Fundamentally, you need to evaluate your strengths and weaknesses and determine if your capabilities are a good match for the requirements of the assignment. If we simplify things, we can divide these requirements into those that meet tactical objectives and those that meet strategic objectives.

Meeting tactical objectives usually requires the skills you currently have, skills that are well honed. In fact, we suspect that you were chosen for an international assignment precisely because you do so well in your current job; otherwise, you wouldn't be reading this book! Perhaps you were chosen to reduce the cost structure in a foreign operation because you have recently done that in your home country. You should remember, though, that doing a job well in one country may not require the exact same knowledge and skills to accomplish it in another country. To do the same thing overseas may very well require that you know the local language, customer preferences, employee motivations, and so on. So the key here is focusing on the additional knowledge and skill that will be needed beyond that which you already have in order to meet tactical objectives.

Meeting strategic objectives requires certain skills, experiences, and relationships. For example, if a global assignment's primary purposes are to increase headquarters' control of the subsidiary and to increase coordination among subsidiaries, you must have a broad range of experience as well as a wide array of contacts throughout the company. If the strategic objective is transferring innovations from foreign operations to headquarters, or to other subsidiaries, you must have excellent cross-cultural communication skills to access the innovation. Since the information should travel from subsidiary to subsidiary, you must know how to communicate it across many cultures. Finally, if professional development is the strategic purpose of an assignment, then you need to understand the development potential inherent in the assignment and your capabilities for stretching to new levels of competency. While your assignment may accomplish all these strategic objectives, what is most critical is that you fully understand the key strategic purposes of the international assignment and carefully assess the degree to which your skills, knowledge, and experience will accomplish those purposes.

Personal Characteristics for Cross-Cultural Success

While your boss might have chosen you for your technical skills, the key to making those technical skills shine during an international assignment is complementing them with sophisticated cross-cultural competencies. In our consulting, research, and experience as expatriates, we have found six key cross-cultural skills that make a significant difference in an expatriate's effectiveness: cultural flexibility, cosmopolitan perspective, sociability, willingness to communicate, conflict-resolution style, and leadership approach.

Cultural Flexibility. Cultural flexibility is your ability to replace activities enjoyed at home with new activities in the foreign country. As an expatriate, you must be willing to try new things such as new foods, new sports, new forms of recreation, or new ways of traveling. For example, when you visit Japan, are you willing to try *sushi* or *yakisoba* instead of a Big Mac and fries? Or if Swedes come to Miami, are they willing to substitute *jai alai* for hockey? Opportunities to try something new occur frequently in a foreign culture, and people who are adventurous enough to try new things adjust more effectively to the new culture. In foreign countries, families often can't find the foods they are used to, but discovering new foods and things to do can be fun. The new culture will not be home, but if you can live with that, you will quickly discover the new country's charm.

Cosmopolitan Perspective. This is the ability to see things from others' perspectives, or conversely, the inability to see or accept things from any other perspective than one's own. Your capacity to see things from others' perspectives will make it easier to live and work in a foreign country. How we interpret what is going on around us can significantly impact our adjustment in a foreign assignment—especially if we misinterpret and negatively evaluate the behavior or people when crossing cultural boundaries. For example, a Japanese manager in a negotiation process with a manager from Finland may think that the sound created by the Finn sucking in air through his mouth means that the Finn has a negative response to the deal, but the Finn can actually be communicating agreement by making the same sound that indicates disagreement in Japan. If an American were involved, he or she might wonder if Japanese and Finnish people have breathing problems. Using our own rules for interpreting behavior in other cultures often leads us to *mis*interpret actions and intentions. As a result, expatriates who are less rigid in their evaluations of the "rightness" and "wrongness" of others' behavior are more likely to succeed when working overseas. When people see their own way as the only "right" way, this characteristic is often called *ethnocentricity*. The power of ethnocentricity is quite real: expatriates and spouses around the world tell us that people on international assignments must be flexible and have open minds. They must be cosmopolitan. They suspend judgment as they approach new situations and are far less likely to criticize behavior in the new culture. As a result, they adjust much better to the new environment.

Sociability. Sociability is your ability to establish relationships with host nationals, and thereby learn new cultural road maps and traffic signals. It also reflects your ease at meeting and getting acquainted with new people, especially foreigners. Your approach to social situations, or the ability to establish relationships with host nationals, helps you learn critical new cultural road maps and traffic signals. Although sociability may not necessarily have a large impact on professional success in your home country, it is essential for an overseas assignment.

Willingness to Communicate. Willingness to communicate reflects your desire to communicate with host nationals and persist at understanding and trying to be understood—even when initial attempts don't work. Clearly, knowing the local language can be vital to effective cross-cultural adjustment and work effectiveness. But after you attain a minimum level of language proficiency, your confidence and willingness to communicate with foreign nationals becomes even more critical to your success. While this characteristic may seem obvious, many expatriates are simply unwilling to try to connect with host-country nationals. Instead, they rely on subordinates and translators to communicate the "necessary information" instead of engaging in genuine two-way conversations. An unwillingness to communicate can ultimately frustrate the strategic purposes of the assignment, since it will be difficult to fully coordinate, control, and transfer innovations without effective communication.

The importance of wanting to communicate is also relevant to spouses overseas, since they often have to work even harder to initiate and develop social relationships, especially when others may not want to communicate with them. For example, one spouse told us, "During both of my global assignments, I have not once received a warm welcome or strong social support from other bank wives. I knew I would have to build my own life overseas, but I expected the first steps to be taken by others in England. My advice to future expatriate spouses? Be prepared and willing to develop contacts and friendships from day one."

Conflict-Resolution Style. Conflict-resolution style is the ability to resolve interpersonal and business conflicts effectively by focusing on both the needs and objectives of the other party, as well as one's own. When people are assigned to work in a new country, they encounter customs, beliefs, attitudes, ideas, values, and actions that differ from those of their home country. Naturally, these differences lead to increased levels of stress and conflict. Your ability to resolve conflict collaboratively is valuable when approaching the endless conflicts, stresses, and differences encountered when living and working in a foreign country. In fact, a collaborative conflict-resolution approach works well in most cultures.

Leadership Approach. Leadership styles can have a significant impact on expatriate effectiveness. You need the ability to focus both on developing and working effectively with and through others, and the capacity to get the job done and achieve the desired results. While managers from different countries and cultures use a variety of leadership styles, your leadership style is key to gaining the trust of fellow employees by accomplishing tasks and building people during the international assignment. While people who focus on getting things done can be successful in their home culture, this approach rarely is successful when crossing cultural borders because things are often not done the same way; and without a strong emphasis on understanding others, you have no way to learn how to accomplish in the new culture what you need to accomplish.   Conversely,   simply   focusing   on understanding others is also not a successful leadership approach overseas. While you do need to understand others, results are also critical. So while more "unidimensional" (just focusing on tasks or just focusing on people) might be effective leadership styles in your home country, a more multidimensional leadership approach is required when working overseas.

Assessing Personal Cross-Cultural Strengths and Weaknesses

Throughout the world, the selection of expatriates relies heavily on interviews. Interviews, however, are not necessarily the most effective way for you to assess your cross-cultural strengths and weaknesses. You can use a variety of tools to assess your competencies, including assessment centers and surveys.

Survey instruments (or questionnaires) can give you valuable insights into your strengths and weaknesses, and the results can be helpful decision-making guides. Individual characteristics such as conflict-resolution style or willingness to communicate can be reliably assessed with standardized psychological tests. In our own work with multinational firms, we have developed a standardized test that assesses several important selection criteria for global assignments. The Global Assignment Preparedness Survey (G–A–P–S™) is an assessment tool designed to give individuals feedback on their strengths and weaknesses relative to characteristics that influence success or failure in international assignments. It helps you assess yourself along the six critical dimensions we discussed earlier: cultural flexibility, cosmopolitan perspective, sociability, willingness to communicate, conflict-resolution style, and leadership approach. These characteristics significantly influence the success of an expatriate. As a consequence, assessing this area is key for success in overseas assignments.

The development of this assessment instrument began over ten years ago with an exhaustive review of the research literature on personal factors that affect cross-cultural adjustment, international assignment success, and job performance. This theoretical work led us to identify six personal characteristics that influence cross-cultural adjustment and job performance in international assignments. The results of our studies show a significant relationship between the dimensions measured in the G–A–P–S™ instrument before they took international assignments and critical business outcomes after they arrived in the assignment (such as cross-cultural adjustment, on-the-job performance, and commitment to stay in the assignment).

WOMEN EXPATRIATES SUCCEED OVERSEAS

The percentage of women expatriates from U.S. companies, though still small, has grown from 3% to approximately 10% over the last several years. Even though women make up nearly 40% of all managers in the U.S., they have represented only a small percentage of the international assignee population. Companies often assumed that women would not be as successful as men or that their spouse worked and therefore would not be willing to relocate. Both assumptions turn out to be wrong. Research consistently shows that women perform just as well as men do, both during and after global assignments. This is even true for female expatriates in traditionally male-dominated societies like Japan and Korea. For example, a female executive sent to Japan from IBM corporate headquarters in the United States is seen by the Japanese first as a company representative, second as a foreigner, and third as a woman. The first two factors add up to the expatriate's gender becoming a non-issue for most Japanese businessmen. Even if foreigners are not used to having women in the workplace, this cultural bias does not necessarily result in performance problems for female expatriates. Furthermore, expatriates in dual-career situations are just as likely as single-career couples to complete global assignments and perform effectively after returning home.

MAKING THE RIGHT MATCH WORK FOR YOU

The entire selection decision should help you create realistic expectations about work and life in the foreign country, assess your professional and cross-cultural competencies, and determine your unique spouse and family needs. We cannot overemphasize the importance of having a realistic preview of the job and of living overseas, and then determining your fit with that new work and living context. If there is a good fit, an international assignment can be a rewarding personal, family, and professional experience.

Chapter Three

What Are the Logistics of the Move?

Once you've made the decision to go, getting all the logistics organized is a major undertaking. The companion workbook has a variety of lists and exercises you can use to keep track of various tasks you need to take care of for your specific assignment and the relevant time tables. Because many of the specific details depend on where you are going, in this chapter we will simply walk through the basic issues concerning the logistics of the move.

GETTING ORGANIZED

In getting organized, it may seem as though you have an endless list of things to check on, information to gather, decisions to make, and paperwork to complete. The key in getting all of it organized is making sure that it is organized well enough so that you are not going over things endlessly in your mind and using up valuable mental energy reviewing and re-reviewing your "to do" list. For some people, this means having a list of all the tasks to be done, the deadline by which they need to be done, and who is assigned responsibility for each task. They end up with a major "pert chart" for logistics. You may not need to take such an elaborate approach, but from interviews with hundreds of experienced expatriates, we can safely say that it is better to be overorganized with charts and lists than underorganized.

You personally will be under a lot of stress. If you are married or have a family, they will be experiencing their own stress and strain in getting ready for the move. Poorly organized logistics can be at times the proverbial "straw that breaks the camel's back": that extra little source of stress, causing you to blow up at home or work over something small and silly, forcing you to backtrack, apologize, and try to repair the damage. Here's what one expatriate recalled:

> I didn't think that the stress of the move would be that great. I was busy at work and didn't bother getting organized, but knew I should. It didn't really dawn on me until one day my little girl asked me to fix her doll house. I lost it. I told her I didn't have time to fix the damn doll house, that there were a lot more important things to do. Her eyes welled up with these gut-wrenching crocodile tears, and I felt horrible. All she wanted was to make sure her doll house was ready for the move. After that I realized that I needed to sit down with the family and put together a plan.

The point is that while different people organize things differently, and therefore there is no "one best way" to organize, organizing and tracking the various issues we discuss in this next section and throughout this chapter are critical for everyone.

Change of Address

You're moving to Timbuktu; who do you need to tell? You will be amazed at the number of people and companies you need to inform of your change of address.

Let's start with the post office. If you live in the U.S. you should complete its standard change of address form—be aware that it will not forward mail to an international address. Therefore, you will need to provide a new domestic address. This most likely will be your company or a personal mail service provider.

Many companies will allow you to direct your mail to the company mailroom, and then they forward it to you on a regular schedule. If your company does not offer this service, you may want to check with companies such as Personal Mail International (Tel: 201-927-4722) that provide international mail forwarding services.

In either case, you will need to notify a variety of people and companies about your move. The companion workbook contains some sample form letters that you can use or adapt to suit your needs. The more important people and companies to inform of your move are listed below:

- **Accountant**—Not that you would forget to inform your accountant, but you wouldn't want to surprise her with a letter from Fiji saying, "By the way, I moved. And I won't be back for three years."

- **Alumni Organizations**—Though you may want to disappear to avoid donation requests, there may be alumni chapters in the country to which you are moving that can serve as useful support and networking organizations.

- **Banks**—it's safest to send a separate letter to each department (e.g., checking, savings, loan, etc.), because there is no guarantee that one letter will be coordinated across all departments.

- **Charge Cards**—You'll probably want to simply cancel department store cards and most gasoline charge cards (e.g., BP, Exxon, Mobil, Shell, etc.) In the case of gas cards, even though most of the major oil companies have service stations the world over, their charge card systems often vary country to country.

- **Church**—If you are involved in a church, let the minister know of the move and your new address. The minister may also be able to help you with information on church locations, services, etc., in your new location.

- **Credit Cards**—While cards such as American Express, Master Card, and Visa can be used the world over, you don't want long delays in receiving your billing statements so contact them to avoid undesired late payments and penalties.

- **Friends**—Pull out your holiday card list, or something like that, and send everyone a brief letter informing them of your move. You don't want one friend saying to another, "You know I haven't heard from ____ for a while." "Oh, that's because they moved to Timbuktu. I'm surprised they didn't let you know."

- **Insurance Companies**—Alert those companies with which you have your life, health, automobile, home, or other policies.

- **Lawyers**—They need to know where to reach you.

- **Stockbroker/Mutual Funds**—If you can, it's best to give them a domestic address.

In addition to these people and companies that you inform about your change of address, don't forget people and companies with whom you need to cancel services. Some of these include the following:

- **Furnace oil company**

- **Garbage collector**

- **Magazine subscriptions**

- **Newspapers**

- **Pest control**

- **Utilities**

Banking

Most expatriates suggest having an account with a major bank with worldwide operations, such as Citibank or Bank of America, if such is possible. This can greatly facilitate the flow of funds and the consistency of service you receive.

A critical thing to consider if you are married is whether to have joint or separate accounts. Experienced expatriates note that while having separate accounts at home is typically no problem, it can be a problem overseas. This is because many expatriate assignments involve considerably more travel than domestic assignments. Thus one person may be traveling when funds need to be transferred, and separate accounts become potentially inconvenient.

If you are a non-US citizen going to the United States, be sure you have a widely accepted credit card (American Express, Visa, or Master Card) before you arrive.

Obtaining a credit card in the U.S. without a credit history can be problematic.

Cars

The advice of most expatriates is that unless you have an antique car or one you plan to keep your entire lifetime, sell your cars before you leave. Unless they are professionally prepared for a three-to five-year storage, they will not do well in storage. You may wonder about shipping your car to the country of your assignment. Most expatriates advise against this. Simple things like parts and mechanics familiar with your make and model of car can be hard to find. Finally, because nearly all cars depreciate over time (even ones in storage), financially you are better off selling your car and investing the cash rather than letting that cash simply depreciate.

Driver's Licenses

In many countries a U.S. driver's license will be recognized and valid. However, for a fee of around $10 you can get an international driver's license through organizations such as the American Automobile Association or "Triple A" (AAA, telephone 1-888-926-4222). If your driver's license is due to expire while you are overseas, you may want to renew it before you go. In many cases this can be done easily through the mail.

Inventories

Although difficult, household and personal inventories are absolutely essential. You will want not only a list of all your household items, but pictures and even videos of major or expensive items (antique china cabinet, jewelry, furs, etc.) You will need this inventory for insurance purposes. Even if you move everything, you will need the inventory for your moving insurance. If you decide to leave some things in storage, you will need the inventory for your storage insurance.

However, if you view the creation of a household inventory as simply a task you have to do for insurance purposes, it can become a boring undertaking. Experienced expatriates recommend trying to attach other motivations to this activity. One of the most frequently recommended is using the creation of a household inventory as a great opportunity to sort through things and "clean house." If you are moving to a location with conditions that prevent you from bringing all of your belongings (such as home size or weather and climate), now may be the time to decide on things you can throw away, donate, or sell. Most of us have a tendency to accumulate "stuff," and taking an inventory of all the stuff you have may be a great time to sort through it so that you don't go to the time and expense of moving or storing things you don't really want or need anymore.

In addition to a household inventory, you will need to create, or at least update, your personal inventory. The companion workbook provides a worksheet on which you can record personal inventory items. Things that need to go in this personal and family inventory include the following:

- **Bank Account**—including account numbers, bank address, customer service telephone number and representative name.

- **Credit Cards**—including account numbers, addresses, customer service telephone numbers, lost or stolen department numbers.

- **Insurance Policies** — including policy numbers, company addresses, customer service telephone numbers and agents' names.

- **Legal Documents** — including will, real estate deeds, car titles, and so on. Location of these documents and your authorized agent name (such as your lawyer), address, and telephone number.

- **Loan Accounts** — including account numbers, addresses, customer service telephone numbers and representatives' names.

- **Passport** — including passport number for you and any family members, issuance date, expiration date, issuing agency and location, service telephone number in your home country and country of assignment.

- **Safety Deposit Box** — including account number, address, authorized agents, customer service telephone number.

- **Government Identification** — including numbers (such as social security) for you and any family members, address, customer service telephone number.

- **Stocks and bonds** — including brokerage account numbers, company addresses, customer service telephone numbers and brokers' names.

Keep a copy of this personal inventory with you and also leave a copy with a trusted agent (family member, lawyer, etc.) While creating such a personal inventory may seem time-consuming, trying to find account numbers, telephone numbers, and addresses when you are thousands of miles away is much more difficult.

Insurance

While we have already mentioned some of these things, make sure you understand the insurance coverage of your household shipments, as well as medical and dental insurance. Check to make sure that your current life and disability insurance covers you while you are living and working in a foreign country. Although we recommend selling your cars, if you decide to store your car(s), make sure you have insurance to cover them if they are stolen or damaged. Also, make sure you have adequate insurance coverage for any items you keep in storage during your assignment.

Medical and Dental

Most companies will have medical and dental insurance policies for their international assignees. This may take the form of an international policy designed specifically for expatriates, subscription to the national policy and plan in the host country, or a combination of both. Whatever the case, it is important that you understand fully and have a copy of the policy.

In addition, you will need to get a copy of your personal medical and dental records, and those of your family. If you are taking any prescription medicine, make sure you have a typed copy (not your doctor's illegible handwriting) of the prescription signed by your doctor. While your doctor's prescription is unlikely to be valid in a foreign country, at least the doctor there will know exactly what you were taking back home. Also, if you are taking any prescription medicine, consult your doctor about the likelihood of obtaining the medication in the country of assignment and discuss the need or option of taking extra quantities with you. If you do take medications with you, make sure you leave them in their original containers with their original labels. You don't want to try to explain to a customs officer that what's in the unmarked bottle is really prescription.

If you or anyone in you family wears corrective lenses, make sure you have a copy of the prescription. Carry this prescription with you in case anything happens to your glasses or contacts during the trip or soon after your arrival in the assignment.

Passports and Visas

You can count on needing a passport for yourself and any family members. Within the United States there are thirteen different regional passport agencies. In addition, passport offices are attached to many post offices in large cities. If you do not have a passport, you will need to appear in person to get one. Otherwise, you can apply by mail if you have been issued a passport within the last twelve years and your old passport was not issued to you while you were age sixteen or younger. If you need to apply in person, you will need proof of U.S. citizenship and proof of identity. Birth certificates are the most common form of citizen documentation. However, to avoid problems, try to obtain a certified birth certificate. If you are a naturalized citizen, you will need to bring your Certificate of Naturalization. If you were born to a U.S. citizen parent but outside the U.S., you will need a Report of Birth Abroad of a Citizen of the U.S.A. Proof of identify typically requires a driver's license, or government identify card that includes a photograph. Credit cards, social security cards, and so on are not valid forms of identify verification for passport offices. Each member of the family, including babies, must have his or her own passport. Each family member over the age of thirteen must appear in person to apply.

While you will need to have your passport when you travel to your assignment and as you travel to various countries while on assignment, once inside a foreign country, do not carry your passport with you, even if you are told that you must always have your passport on you. Instead, keep your passport in a safe in your new home overseas or in the hotel safe when you're traveling, and carry with you a photocopy of the two pages that include your picture, issuing authority, expiration dates, and so on. While a lost passport can be replaced, it is not a simple process—particularly when traveling on a tight business schedule.

Visas are required in many countries. Visas are issued by the country to which you are traveling. Typically, you will apply for a visa prior to entering the country by sending in the necessary forms to the nearest consulate. Most countries to which you would move have consulate offices in the U.S. Sometimes you need to move to the country before proper work visas can be issued. Take care. If you enter a country on a tourist visa, often the household goods that you shipped will be held up until you receive a proper visa.

If you or your spouse gives birth to a child in a foreign country, immediately apply for a passport and any necessary visas for that child. Several families we know have given birth to a new son or daughter, traveled with the new baby outside the country, and then tried to return, only to be denied reentrance because the baby was "undocumented."

The companion workbook has a variety of references for U.S. citizens relative to passport offices, foreign consulates, and other government agencies that may be of use to you.

It also contains a list of other types of permits and documentation that can be required in some countries, such as police certification of good standing, medical certificate of good health, certificates of proper inoculation and immunization, and so on.

Pets

For many of us, certain pets are like members of the family. We could no more think of moving to a foreign country without them than we could think of leaving young children behind. However, early in the process, check carefully into restrictions and regulations. In some countries, the quarantine period can be amazingly long. For example, in Australia, the quarantine period for dogs and other pets can be six months. In this case, might your beloved pet not be better off staying at home with a friend or relative? Other things to check into include required visas for pets, medical records, shots and immunizations, duties that must be paid, and certificates of health. Make sure you know what day your pet will arrive and if the customs office is open on that day. Otherwise, your pet may go neglected until the office opens. Also talk with the airlines about their policies and facilities for transporting pets. Finally, you might consider using a specialized "pet mover." These service providers facilitate the actual pet move and many expatriates have found their help invaluable.

Once you learn how your pets will have to travel to the foreign country and what conditions they will encounter during the trip and upon arrival, you may decide that it's best for them to stay at home. While we do not want to create the impression that taking pets with you is a bad idea — psychologically it can be a very good one — we do want to convey that it is something you need to investigate early and thoroughly. We stress this warning because too often we have seen individuals and families get caught up in everything else and discover various restrictions and requirements the hard way at the last minute.

Pictures

You will need pictures of you and any family members for a variety of purposes—passports, visas, alien registration cards, work permits, and so on. To be safe, take about a dozen passport-size pictures for yourself and any family members. If this seems like too many, keep in mind that visas, alien registration cards, etc., typically require two pictures. It only takes six such applications to use up a dozen pictures.

Power of Attorney

"Power of Attorney" is a legal document that allows an agent (someone other than yourself) to act either broadly or in narrowly specified ways on your behalf. In some cases you will need to grant power of attorney because you were unable to complete everything you needed to before moving, such as selling your car, closing on the sale of your house, finding renters for your home, and so on. To the extent that you know the specific tasks that need to be carried out, the power of attorney should specify them. You should consult your attorney before granting a general power of attorney to someone, because courts can interpret these powers broadly, and such an empowered individual could trade stocks, sell assets, etc. In any case, the exact nature of power of attorney can vary from area to area (such as how it needs to be notarized, canceled, and so on), so you should consult an attorney before you grant power of attorney—limited or general—to your attorney or anyone else.

Wills and Trusts

You should make sure that your will is current, that a notarized and legal copy is held by your attorney, and that relevant instructions are held by your attorney, a trusted family member, or friend. While terminal illness, accident, or anything else dire is far from your mind, if the worst should happen, you should make sure that your wishes are clearly spelled out and accessible if needed. If something should happen to you while overseas, you should spell out in an updated will how you want your funeral and other arrangements to be handled. If you have minor children, specify a legal guardian and see that that individual has a notarized copy of the document. In some cases, only a legal guardian can take children out of a country.

HOUSING

Some of the most important decisions you will make concern housing. Will you sell or rent your home? Where will you live while overseas? In this section, we pass on the advice of experienced expatriates and provide some important questions for you to ask of yourself and others to help you make critical housing decisions.

Selling or Renting Your Home

Deciding whether to sell your home or rent it out while you are away is one of the most critical decisions you will make. If you talk to expatriates who went overseas during high inflation times, they will invariably tell you that you should never sell your home. This is primarily because many of them found that in their absence, inflation had sent housing prices skyward, and they were priced out of the market because they sold their home before they left and were unable to keep up with inflation through the appreciating value of their home. If you talk to someone who went abroad during low inflation times, they are likely to give you the exact opposite advice. So how should you decide?

First, you need to talk with a tax accountant or real estate lawyer concerning the specific tax implications of selling your home. This is especially critical for any capital gains you might acquire from selling the home. Since laws and regulations in this area change regularly (almost every year it seems), be sure to check with someone who will carefully review the tax implications with you.

Assuming that the tax implications don't determine the selling or renting of your home, what else should you consider?   First, you will want to consider the tax implications of renting your home.   Rent income is typically taxable, but a variety of expenses are tax deductible. To understand all the implications, you should thoroughly explore this issue with a qualified individual.

In addition, you may want to consider the likelihood that once your international assignment is over, you will (or want to) return to your old city, neighborhood, and home. If you think this is unlikely, then tax and other considerations should probably dominate your decision. If, however, you think there is a high probability, then you should seriously factor in the emotional and psychological value of returning to your old home. You may decide that these benefits outweigh any costs associated with renting your house while you are away.

If you decide to rent your house, experienced expatriates strongly advise against trying to be the landlord yourself. You will be too far away and too busy to put up with all the headaches of playing landlord. They recommend hiring a professional property management agent to handle things for you. While you normally will have to pay a commission to the property management company (about 15% of the rent), the headaches you'll avoid are probably worth it. However, make sure you understand if the fee is on gross or net rent, and who is responsible for collecting back rent, repairs and maintenance, etc. Whatever the agreement, be psychologically prepared for repairs and "sprucing up" when you move back home. Several expatriates we interviewed had to spend upwards of $10,000 to get their home into the shape they wanted, even though they were satisfied with the professionalism of the property management company and agent they used while overseas.

Whether you decide to sell or rent your house, the companion workbook has a set of steps to take, specific questions to ask and get answered, and mistakes to avoid.

Finding a Place Overseas

Next to what you decide relative to your house back home, your housing decision overseas is probably the most critical logistical one you will make. However, as many experienced expatriates will tell you, housing conditions vary from country to country, and relatively few countries have conditions similar to those in your home country. So from the outset expect things to be different.

Before you get deep into a search for a new home overseas, make sure you thoroughly understand your company's housing policies. Know what your allowance is, if any. Some companies have leased or purchased homes or apartments, and you will need to live in one of these predetermined locations or pay for alternative housing on your own.

Housing Considerations

Many of the housing considerations you will explore overseas are the same as you would examine at home. These include things such as distance and time from work, location and quality of schools, convenience of shopping, composition of neighbors (older, younger, with kids, etc.), and so on. If you have children, pay special attention to the location and travel convenience of the school(s) your children will attend and the location of your house. The companion workbook provides a simple exercise for you to discuss and weigh the various criteria you may want to consider in selecting a house or apartment. It also contains some more specific questions you may want to consider in your housing decision.

Once you finally start looking at housing, experienced expatriates recommend starting with a broad set of alternatives. Because housing conditions and descriptions can be so different in other countries, you will save time in the end by beginning with an array of housing alternatives that cover the spectrum. This will allow you to determine more quickly what your budget will really buy, and what compromises you may have to accept. Expatriates also recommend this approach because many agents that have dealt with expatriates in the past develop stereotypes of what "Germans" or "Americans" like. You may or may not fit that preconceived notion. We have known many individuals and families who selected housing that their agent originally didn't want or think to show them. Starting with a broad spectrum will also help you come to understand what specific terms and conditions mean in that country. For example, a "combined kitchen/living room" may actually mean that you have about 30 square feet of kitchen space and literally must eat standing over the stove or in the living room. It will give you an idea of what "furnished" and "unfurnished" mean. In some countries, "unfurnished" means that it doesn't even have appliances such as a stove or refrigerator. To be safe, you should tell yourself that you do not know what any of the typical housing terms or descriptions mean, because in many cases, you won't. You'll think you know what "unfurnished" means, but you'll be wrong. Don't assume. Instead, spend at least one day getting a clear idea of the entire spectrum from top to bottom.

Agent Considerations

If your company does not predetermine your housing, you will likely use an agent to help you locate and select your new home. You will want to consider several things in selecting and working with an agent. The following recommendations have consistently been put forward by experienced expatriates we have interviewed over the years:

- **Experience** — While you may not have the exact preferences as other expatriates, you are likely to share some common desires and expectations. An agent experienced in working with foreigners can save you significant time and energy.

- **Reputation** — Ask others in your company or in other companies who they have used or what their experience was with a particular company or agent you are thinking of using.

- **Language** — Unless you speak the local language well, you will need an agent with excellent skills in your native language. With housing, the devil is in the details, so you need an agent who can talk to you clearly about the details of the lease, the landlord, the location, etc.

Settling In Considerations

In many cases, companies actually sign the lease. If they do, they will undoubtedly have someone review and approve the lease. Make sure that this happens and that you know what your obligations are, even if you are not the signer of the lease.

If you personally sign the lease, do not do so until you have had legal counsel review the lease with you. Just as housing terms may not mean the same thing in a foreign country as they do at home, neither may the legal terms or the legal framework within which they are set.

Don't move in until the lease has been reviewed and approved, or until you have inspected the house and are satisfied that its condition meets with what you agreed to. For example, you may have negotiated for the carpets to be cleaned, walls painted, or floors cleaned. Do not move in until these things have been completed. Not only will it be difficult to get them done after you've moved in, but the landlord may not be obligated to do so. Moving in may be tantamount to waving the "premove-in" alterations or repairs agreed to in the lease.

As with any new home, make sure you understand how long it will take to get utilities (especially phone service in some countries) hooked up. The last thing you want is to move in and have to wait days for the water, electricity, or gas to be turned on. In some countries, it can take weeks and even months to get certain utilities in your home.

PACKING AND MOVING

Packing and moving can be exciting, depressing, chaotic, scary, and fun—all at the same time. It is both an emotional and an intellectual activity. As we mentioned, you need to be organized, but at the same time you need to acknowledge and anticipate that your own emotions and those of any family members will be stirred up in the process.

In this section we examine the basics of packing and moving. In the companion workbook, we provide more detailed check lists and steps to take. Whether you are using just this book or using it in combination with the workbook, the key thing to keep in mind is that you can probably never be too organized or start too early.

The Company Policy

Unless you are one of the first expatriates in your company, your company will no doubt have a policy relative to moving overseas. That policy may have poundage limits, absolute expense limits, preferred providers, and special allowances. Get a copy of the policy as early as possible and clarify any questions you have with representatives within the company.

Movers

Your company may have a preferred provider agreement with a moving company. If so, meet with a representative of that company as early as you can. If you are free to choose your mover, ask others who they have used and what their experience was. In addition, you should use several key criteria in selecting a mover:

- **General International Experience**—How many people did the mover relocate from the U.S. to international locations? How long has the mover been doing international relocations?

- **Specific Country Experience**—Has the mover ever moved anyone to the country of your assignment? How many? How recently? Would the mover provide references for these specific moves? Is there a dedicated agent in the assignment country?

- **Openness to Questions**—How open and receptive are the company and its representative(s) to the questions above? This will give you a great indication of how well they will work with you and answer a myriad of more specific questions.

Once you have a good idea of which company you might use, you may want to ask a variety of specific questions before finalizing your decision. Here are just a few to consider and that will hopefully spark others related to your specific situation:

- **Containerization**—Where will your goods be containerized? Is the facility indoors or out? Are the containers waterproof?

- **Cost Estimates**—How will cost estimates be determined? When? How much can actual costs differ from estimates?

- **Customs**—How familiar is the mover with customs in the country of assignment? How long does it typically take goods to clear customs?

- **Insurance**—What are the limitations of the insurance? Does it cover packing, shipment, delivery?

- **Legal Documents**—What documents are needed for customs? Are work visas required for receiving goods?

- **Packers**—What is the company's level of experience? Does it have full-time employees or contract hires?

- **Packing Time**—How long will packing take? Can fewer packers be used over a longer period so that you can better monitor their activity?

- **Payment**—How and when is payment to be made? How are reimbursements for damage handled? What is the average number of claims? What is the average length of time for claims to be resolved?

- **Receiving Agents**—Who is the receiving agent? How much experience does the mover have with the agent? How experienced is the agent?

- **Restrictions**—What sort of items are restricted (guns, plants, magazines, medicines, etc.), rationed (e.g., one TV, one refrigerator, etc.), or taxed?

- **Special Handling**—What experience does the mover have with special handling of items, such as pianos, art, or antiques? What are the special handling practices?

- **Storage**—What storage advice can the mover provide? Is the mover experienced at preparing goods for long-term storage?

- **Shipping Time**—How long will it take for the goods to be shipped, received, and delivered? What guarantees does the mover provide? What compensation is provided for late shipments?

Once you've asked these and other questions, you should have a good idea of how capable the mover is and how comfortable you will be working with that mover. Keep in mind that you are the customer and that the movers are moving not just household items, but things that are part of your home. Be sure you are confident and comfortable before engaging any mover.

In-Country Assistance

Make sure you have a good understanding of your company's in-country assistance policies. These cover everything from real-estate agents to housing and furniture allowances. Once you settle into a house, your company can help with locating and paying for a "destination service." Destination service providers often help you with information about schools, doctors, hospitals, churches, social clubs, cultural activities, and so on. The best services offer excellent information on critical issues such as quality medical care and doctors. While getting your household packed up and moved is important, you need to make sure you have an idea of what help you will or won't have in getting settled in.

Unpacking

Finally, your stuff has arrived! Don't be surprised if you have to go down to the customs office personally to receive the shipment, or if you need your passport, working permit, signed lease, shipping documents, or residency permit. Your mover should know what documents you will need and what procedures you'll need to follow.

Make sure that you double-check your inventory sheet against the boxes and items delivered and open every box to check for obvious damage. Although most shippers and insurance give you several days after delivery to file any damage or loss claims, you are better off making note of obvious lost or damaged goods as they are delivered.

Have a plan worked out in advance as to which boxes and items go in which rooms. As the items come in, direct them to the appropriate room. Keep in mind that depending on your country of assignment, the workers likely won't speak your native language. Expatriates we have interviewed suggest putting a number or letter above the door of each room. This way you can simply look at a box, find it on your inventory sheet, and then direct the worker to "Room A."

Like packing, many experienced expatriates recommend using fewer workers and taking longer so that you can be sure of your inventory, initial condition of items, and the placement of items in the rooms they belong. Having a dozen workers hauling boxes and furniture in a steady stream is likely to cause you to just throw up your hands and tell them to "put it anywhere." Even though you'll spend a little extra time up front by using fewer workers to haul your goods in, you'll spend less time overall unpacking than if you let a mass of workers unload your goods in a frenzy.

Make sure you know if it is customary to tip the movers or not, and if so, how much is typical? Your mover, agent, or someone in the office should be able to help you with this one.

Settling In

Once you have unpacked and checked overall damage, you'll begin the process of settling in. If you've completed the "What Personal Items to Bring" exercise in the companion workbook, you'll have a set of personal things that will help turn your house into your new home. To the extent you can, try to get these items up early in the unpacking process.

If you have children, let them help unpack their rooms and get them set up as early as possible. Children are fairly resilient, but having their room set up with a few important personal items can go a long way to helping them settle in and feel a bit more secure.

Experienced expatriates recommend attending some cultural or social event as early as possible—even before you are completely settled in.   Otherwise, you risk isolating yourself and family members with the very legitimate, but ultimately "unhelpful" excuse that you will become more involved as soon as you get settled in. The problem is that settling in can take months, and in the meantime you have established a pattern of isolation and uninvolvement that is difficult to break. Expatriates advise, "Don't even let this pattern get started!"

RETURNING HOME

Later in this book we talk extensively about repatriation and the challenges of making it successful. However, here we want to mention a few logistic issues to keep in mind.

- **Cars**—There are several questions to ask concerning the sale of a car you might have purchased during your assignment. What are the taxes and legal "bill of sale" documents? Do license plates need to be returned to the government agency or left with the car? Are there rebates owed to you for unused portions of road taxes or registration fees? If you decide to import a car back into your home country, take care. Make sure you deal with a knowledgeable agent, or you may find your nice Mercedes is stuck in customs for months because it doesn't meet local emission standards.

- **Moving Documents**—Make sure you get these in advance. If the mover is locally based, you may need to get the contract translated.

- **Moving Sale**—In many countries, "moving sales" are permitted, while in other countries, such as Japan, they are very uncommon. How and when are they typically done? Is it done quietly among a network of friends and other expatriates, or openly with signs out in front of your home?

- **Packing**—Many of the packing concerns previously discussed apply here as well, but be aware that packing approaches, standards, and materials may be different than you expect. Check in advance. Request changes in approaches with which you are not comfortable.

- **Packers**—The packers most likely do not speak your native language. You will need a supervisor who does. Be *fluent* in the language yourself, or have someone there who is. Packers' standards of "tender loving care" may be different, so fewer packers is better so you can monitor things more closely.

- **Paper Work**—What paper work needs to be completed? Is it available in your native language? If not, you'll need to get copies early so you can get them translated.

- **Home Country Customs**— Make sure you are familiar with customs restrictions in your home country so there are no surprises. In the companion workbook we provide a whole section on specific U.S. customs restrictions and policies.

CONCLUSION

Moving is an exciting and challenging experience. Moving halfway around the world can be overwhelming if you are not prepared. A thorough understanding of your company's policies and an experienced mover are probably the two most important things on which you can focus your time and energy. The companion workbook provides all sorts of additional references, check lists, and steps to take. However, the specifics of your assignment country means that no book or workbook can fill in all the details. You will have to do that on your own, but hopefully this book and the workbook have provided a basic set of guidelines and a framework for filling in the details.

Chapter Four

What Are the Financial Considerations?

Money—it's one of the touchiest subjects concerning international assignments. In all our experience we have yet to encounter an expatriate who thought he or she was paid too much or a company that thought it paid too little. In general, expatriates are happy to be paid more and companies are happy to pay less. So how can we address this issue without making what seem to be opposing expatriate and company objectives from clashing even more intensely?

It turns out that if you dig just a little below the surface on both sides, there is much more alignment of expatriate and company objectives than seems to be the case at the surface. Although many expatriates discuss money, when we interviewed successful expatriates at length, money was rarely the center of their decision to accept an international assignment nor was it the sole motivation for completing the assignment. Of hundreds of experienced expatriates, human resource managers, and senior executives we have talked with, they all point out that if money is your main motivator, you will likely be disappointed in what you get out of your assignment.

Money does not buy happiness or success in an international assignment. But at the same time, it can relieve some uncertainty and inconvenience. Consequently, we do not want to create the impression that money is unimportant or that successful expatriates never considered the financial compensation of an assignment. In our interviews and experience, even though money is rarely the most important factor, it is typically named among the top five factors. So we need to examine this important topic, but at the same time we want to caution you about letting money become the sole criterion in your decision to accept or reject an assignment, or become the key benefit you expect from an assignment.

In this chapter we want to first talk briefly about international assignment compensation in the past and how it has changed. Without a proper historical perspective, you may expect compensation that was common in the past, but just isn't likely today.

We also want to talk about both some general approaches to international assignment compensation and some common specific elements. However, because there are almost as many specific policies about compensation and international assignments as there are companies, we cannot hope to answer all your particular questions. What we want to do, however, is provide an overall framework and examine some specific elements of compensation packages that will help you better evaluate and understand your situation.

COMPENSATION IN THE PAST

In the past, compensation was often used to entice people to go off to strange places and harsh environments. In a sense, money was used to buy off various uncertainties and inconveniences.

The most important of the uncertainties was career uncertainty. Twenty or thirty years ago, the career value of an international assignment in Germany or England, let alone Indonesia or China, was quite small in most companies. As a consequence, rather than return to their homeland and a corporate headquarters that did not necessarily value the experience, knowledge, and skills gained from the international assignment, many who found that they liked working abroad simply stayed there. Often they would rotate from one international assignment to the next. At a general level, these cadres of "internationalists" served themselves and the company well. The companies got capable managers willing to live and work in distant places, and the expatriate managers were financially rewarded for their efforts.

In addition to career uncertainty, expatriate compensation in the past was also used to compensate for all sorts of inconveniences. These included housing conditions, medical facilities, and standards of care and service, food, entertainment, education quality for children, and so on that were not what the expatriate would have experienced at home. In many companies, "allowances" (housing, hardship, education, cost of living, etc.) emerged as a way to compensate expatriates monetarily for inconveniences or lower levels in the standard of living. Allowances grew and became a standard component of most compensation packages, in part because of the low level of career value of an international assignment and the low supply of willing assignees. If the inconveniences or hardships the expatriate might face *could not* be compensated through a career payoff, then many expatriates wanted money as compensation. The fact that in years past the supply of quality assignees was slim also put expatriates in a strong bargaining position to ask for various allowances.

These compensation packages were typically negotiated on a case-by-case basis. The size or overall value of the package was primarily a function of the criticality of the position, the supply of capable and willing candidates, and the negotiation savvy and skills of individual assignees. If the company really needed someone in Indonesia, and John Smith was the only person who could do the job and was also willing to go, John was in a great bargaining position from the outset. Add to this good negotiation skills, and John would likely get a great compensation package. We have interviewed a number of these "old-timer" expatriates who made their careers almost entirely overseas and who earned and saved enough that when they retired they were very well off.

To some extent, this left a legacy that international assignments could be a great way to make lots of money. In companies with long histories of international operations, this legacy has been difficult to overcome. However, even in companies new to the international scene, many prospective expatriates have heard stories about "making out financially" on international assignments that essentially stem from this early legacy.

COMPENSATION TODAY

The compensation of expatriates today is quite different from the past. The competitive pressures of a global economy leave little room for anything but essential elements of a compensation package. In addition, while dual careers have limited the number of some capable managers willing and able to accept international assignments, the overall pool of quality candidates has gone up. This is principally because in many organizations, managers can see the career payoff of a stint overseas. In fact, in companies such as ABB, Nestlé or Citicorp, it is virtually impossible to become a senior executive without an international assignment.

So the landscape of compensation for international assignments has changed. In many companies, it has changed dramatically. While the specifics of your company or your particular case may not match the general profile we will discuss, it still should give you a good idea of the various elements of a compensation package and provide an overall framework within which you can evaluate your situation.

Objectives of International Assignment Compensation

Today, international assignment compensation is geared toward two critical objectives: attracting and retaining quality people, and enhancing feelings of being treated fairly. Let's take a brief look at each one of these.

Attract and Retain Quality People

One of the first objectives of international assignment compensation is to attract and retain quality people. Clearly, there are positive and appealing aspects of living and working in a different country and culture, and you should not lose sight of these nonmonetary but important benefits. Still, the fact remains that there are also such things as leaving family, friends, familiar and comfortable living conditions, education and health-care facilities, entertainment and recreation opportunities, favored foods and shopping areas, and so on that you may not be thrilled about. It is natural for you to want some compensation. However, in most cases, it is unrealistic today to expect that all compensation will take the form of money.

We have encountered many expatriates who started out with a strong focus on money as a means of "buying off" the loss of the things left behind. For example, one manager in Jakarta stated, "The normal grocery store here doesn't carry Wheaties, but with enough money, I can get my Wheaties." Enough money may indeed help you "get your Wheaties," but if you don't focus on enjoying the experience, all the Wheaties in the world are not going to make you happy during your assignment.

Still, your firm will need to offer a minimum level of financial compensation to attract a competent and capable person. A certain level of financial compensation is necessary to entice you to go overseas. Hopefully those two points intersect; that is, hopefully what the company is willing to provide and what you are willing to accept coincide. But as we said at the outset of this chapter, even though we will focus on money, do not make money the center of your decision. What you learn from the assignment will be more valuable than all the money you are paid. Keep in mind that because globalization is the wave of the future, the knowledge, experience, and skills you gain will be of value down the road. In addition, the personal and family growth that can come from the experience are also important benefits to keep in focus. So while the compensation needs to be sufficient to attract you to the assignment, and make it possible to stay, it should not be the sole source of your motivation.

Enhance Feelings of Fairness

International assignment compensation is also intended by nearly all companies to make you feel as though you are being treated fairly. Most people feel they are being treated fairly when what they "put in" or contribute and what they "get out" or receive is equitable to other people. For example, if you compared yourself to a peer in your department and felt that you and this other person were performing at virtually the same level, you would no doubt expect quite similar rewards. However, if someone with significantly more responsibilities than you were performing their responsibilities about as well as you were carrying out yours, you would likely *not* expect to receive the same compensation as they would. Why? Because given their significantly greater responsibilities, their contributions are greater. The point is that you do not need to be treated *equally* or the same to feel you are being treated *equitably* or fairly.

Unfortunately, international assignments are fraught with opportunities to make comparisons without complete information or from limited perspectives, and consequently we end up comparing noncomparables. This usually results in feelings of being treated unfairly when it may, in fact, not be the case. For example, international assignment compensation sometimes can create inequity between expatriates who originate from different countries but are assigned to the same location. For example, a country manager in Japan heading up the local office for a large U.S. multinational commented, "I have a German expatriate working two levels below me with a compensation package equal to mine and twice as large as that of a British expatriate one level above her." Even though the company was trying in each case to provide a compensation package that "equalized" the living standards between their home country and the country of the foreign assignment, because the living standards and costs were different in the U.S., Germany, and the U.K., when compared to Japan, the compensation packages created feelings of inequity and being treated unfairly. If you let yourself, you can easily get caught up in these comparisons. Consider the following quote from the spouse of an American expatriate.

> I feel this firm does not really care about its people and their families as well as it should. Everything is done on the "cheap," which makes adjusting to the new country so much harder, which in turn makes their employees even more stressed out. Comparing this assignment to other major New York banks' employees, my company's benefits were extremely substandard and embarrassing! For example, the housing allowances of many people we met were 25% higher than ours. Home-leave airfares were only "economy" in our company, while other firms were "business class." Significantly higher bonuses were given by other firms. My spouse's company has lost and will continue to lose a great many excellent people should it continue to deal in this way.

In this case, the expatriate left the bank after repatriation primarily because he felt he had been treated unfairly.

But let's change the perspective just for a moment. Suppose you were a competent local manager. Local nationals just one level below you are likely to see large gaps between what they contribute and receive compared to what you contribute and the compensation you receive. To hear you complain about having a housing allowance 25% less than someone else's, when they receive no housing allowance at all and live in a house half the size of yours, will not likely make them feel they are being treated fairly either.

So what is our overall advice? Be careful. It is natural to make comparisons, but we rarely have all the details to really know if the comparisons are comparable! We are not saying just take whatever you are offered and be grateful, we are saying that we have not encountered a company yet that deliberately created international assignment compensation packages to treat people unfairly.

BASIC COMPENSATION APPROACHES

In this next section, we provide an overall perspective of some of the more general approaches to international assignment compensation. After we review these general approaches, we will examine some of the specific allowances that, depending on the circumstances, may be relevant to your situation and compensation package.

Balance Sheet Approach

The balance sheet approach is arguably the dominant approach in most countries. The basic objective of this approach is to ensure that expatriates can maintain a standard of living in the country of assignment similar to that which they enjoy in their home country. The figure on the following page provides a rough illustration of how this approach is designed.

Balance Sheet Approach

Approximately Equal Overall Standard of Living

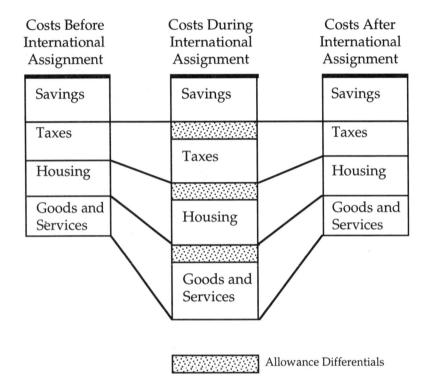

	Costs Before International Assignment	Costs During International Assignment	Costs After International Assignment
	Savings	Savings	Savings
	Taxes	Taxes	Taxes
	Housing	Housing	Housing
	Goods and Services	Goods and Services	Goods and Services

Allowance Differentials

   This approach works relatively well under most conditions. But there are some important situation-specific factors to consider. First, the objective of this approach is to keep the standard of living constant before, during, and after the international assignment. This assumes that individuals leave from their home country and return after the completion of the assignment. This assumption may or may not be true in your case.

Second, this approach works best when most of the firm's expatriates originate from the same country. If expatriates originate from different countries with different standards of living and yet work together in the same country of assignment, the balance sheet approach may actually highlight imbalances. For example, suppose you were from Italy and make less money than a German employee in your company doing the same job in Germany. How upset would you be? As long as you work in Italy and the other employee works in Germany, the differences in pay are unlikely to bother you. But if you and the German employee both take assignments in Japan, the balance sheet approach will likely result in unequal compensation packages. Thus, expatriates of equal responsibility sometimes find it quite difficult to accept unequal compensation packages due to home country cost-of-living differences.

Third, this method is most effective if reliable and detailed figures exist for calculating and comparing standards of living. This detailed information is important because major costs, such as housing, can vary considerably within a country. For example, your housing costs would be different if you lived in San Diego, California versus Provo, Utah. Your housing costs also would be different if you were moving to Tokyo, Japan versus Sendai, Japan. The point is that often companies simply use the average housing or other costs in the home country and host country in determining cost-of-living differentials. This may over- or underrepresent your specific costs.

While the balance sheet approach is not perfect, most experienced expatriates see it as a reasonable and fair approach. However, it works best when employees return to their home countries upon completing their assignment, when most expatriates originate from the same country, and when accurate and specific data exist on the standard of living for both locations.

Parent Country Equivalency Approach

This approach is in many ways quite simple and straightforward. Under this approach, the compensation of all expatriate employees (or all expatriate employees above a certain level) is based on market rates in the country of the company headquarters. For example, a U.S. chemical multinational provides all expatriates, regardless of their country of origin, the same salary and benefits as those in the U.S. This approach reduces the inequality that expatriates from different countries of origin often feel under other approaches when working in the same location.

The effectiveness of this approach is also subject to several important conditions. First, it works best when the home country of the parent firm has relatively high wage and standard of living levels. This is because it is quite simply easier to convince individuals to accept pay scales and standards of living greater but not less than they would have if they remained in their home country.

Second, this approach works best when the expatriate managers on international assignment are career internationalists and move from one foreign assignment to another. This reduces the negative impact that the loss of expatriate compensation creates when individuals return home to countries with lower pay scales and living standards.

Third, this approach works best when there is a relatively small number of managers (50 or fewer) on international assignments in highly globalized companies, such as Citicorp. Paying parent country wages and ensuring parent country living standards, especially when they are high relative to world standards, for a large group of expatriate managers can become very costly. Also, large groups of managers trotting around the globe receiving relative high wages and living standards can often intensify the inequities that local national managers and employees feel, and hurt the expatriate manager's ability to work effectively with local staff.

TAXES

In addition to these basic approaches to compensation, taxes represent the next major aspect of many expatriate compensation packages. However, let us be clear from the outset of this section that expatriates' taxes are a complex issue, and the details and specifics are best handled by experienced professionals. With this said, there are a couple of important issues to understand that will enable you to be better consumers of expatriate tax-consulting or preparation services.

Simplified, there are two general approaches to tax policies and international assignments. The first approach is commonly referred to as *tax protection*. Under this policy, firms reimburse employees for taxes they pay that are in excess of taxes they would have paid had they remained in their country of origin. There are several things to keep in mind. First, many of the extra allowances (which we will cover in more detail shortly) add to your taxable income, and therefore increase your tax obligation. Second, the extra money reimbursed to compensate for these additional taxes can itself become taxable income and generates additional taxes and the need to provide even further reimbursement. Carried to the extreme, this can become a never-ending   cycle   of   compensation   and   tax-reimbursement escalation. Consequently, most firms limit this cycle to one or two rounds.

The second major approach is commonly termed *tax equalization*. The objective of a tax-equalization policy is to see that employees pay *no more* or no *less* than they would have in their home country. Under a tax equalization policy, the tax you would have paid is subtracted from your salary. The firm then pays all actual taxes in the home and host country owed by you.

There are several advantages to the tax equalization approach. First, subtracting the hypothetical home country tax from the total salary reduces the actual taxable income. ORC (Organization Resources Counselors) found differences in how this hypothetical tax was computed. Roughly 25% of U.S. firms estimate it on base salary alone, 54% estimate it on base salary plus bonus, and 8% estimate it on base salary, bonus, and all premiums. Nearly nine out of ten U.S. firms take this approach to taxes. Second, it reduces problems upon repatriation. For example, if you were sent from the U.S. to Saudi Arabia (which has virtually no personal income tax), and were allowed to keep the tax windfall, you would experience a rather significant shock upon repatriating to the U.S. In this scenario, you could easily experience a drop in disposable income of 30-50%.

ALLOWANCES

Once you understand your firm's basic approach to international assignment compensation and taxes, the next major area to consider is allowances. The number and variations of all the allowances offered to expatriate managers are nearly as large and varied as the firms providing them. However, there are a few basic ones, and it is helpful to have a fundamental understanding of them. However, keep in mind that just because we mention a particular allowance, we do not want to create the impression that your firm will or even should provide it. In general, allowances are in decline as part of international assignment compensation packages.

Foreign Service Premiums

A foreign service premium (FSP) is simply money paid in recognition of the employee's and family's willingness to accept and sacrifice to complete an international assignment. This compensation is given in exchange for the inconvenience of living in a foreign land with alien customs, food, weather, transportation systems, education, shopping, and health-care facilities, and for leaving family, friends, and familiar surroundings back home. The policy of most firms that pay this premium is to pay a percentage of base salary, generally between 10 to 25% of base pay. Some firms set a maximum for this premium of, say, $50,000.

Hardship or Site Allowances

A hardship allowance is paid above and beyond a foreign service premium (if an FSP is paid) in recognition of particularly difficult aspects of a specific country or site of the international assignment. These hardships may include things such as physical isolation, climate extremes, political instability and risk, crime, poor standard-of-living conditions due to such things as inadequate housing, education, health care, or food.

Identifying and evaluating hardships and then determining a "fair" compensation value is a difficult task. Most firms take a twofold approach. The first is a simple external market test.   Firms look at the competitive practices of similar firms with expatriate managers serving in the countries or locations in question.   The second test is an internal market test.   Firms simply assess what compensation is necessary to attract quality individuals to the country or site in question.

Cost-of-Living Allowances

Cost-of-living allowances recognize that the costs of equivalent standards of living vary by country.   Most firms pay some form of cost-of-living allowance.   Determining a "fair" cost-of-living allowance requires an assessment of the costs of a comparable "basket of goods" in the country of assignment relative to some comparison country (usually the country of origin).   If the country of assignment costs more than the comparison country, a cost-of-living adjustment is made.   If the cost of living in the country of assignment is less than that of the comparison country, very few European or U.S. firms make *negative* adjustments.

Suppose you were being transferred from Los Angeles to Paris and it was determined that it cost a single individual without family 65% more to live in Paris than in Los Angeles.   If 60% of your $100,000 salary was spendable income (goods and services) and the remaining 40% was disposable income (taxes, savings, and so on), your cost-of-living differential would be $39,000.   The calculation is straightforward:

- Spendable income in Los Angeles =
    $100,000 salary × 60% or $60,000

- Equivalent spendable income in Paris =

  $60,000 × 1.65 (living in Paris is 65% more expensive than living in Los Angeles) = $99,000

- Adjustment of $39,000 for living in Paris

  ($99,000–$60,000=$39,000)

In thinking about any cost-of-living adjustment, you should consider four related factors. First, what is the rate of inflation in both countries? Second, if inflation is high in one country but low in the other, how recently were the original cost-of-living comparisons made? Third, if inflation is high in the country of assignment, how often will cost-of-living adjustments be made? Fourth, is the currency exchange rate controlled by the government? To understand why these factors are important, suppose you were going to Venezuela and the annual inflation rate were 120%. If the original cost-of-living comparisons were made several months ago, they would not accurately represent current living costs in the country. If the exchange rate is controlled by the government, generally it will not represent the true value of the currency. It will overvalue the local currency. Combined with cost-of-living adjustments made only twice a year, you will receive fewer *Bolivar* than needed to keep up with the rate of inflation and cost of living. In the companion workbook, we provide exercises that help you better understand the implications of foreign exchange and inflation in your particular situation.

Housing Allowances

In many parts of the world, housing allowances have become the single most expensive allowance in expatriate compensation packages. For example, apartments in Hong

Kong and Tokyo can easily cost $5,000 to $10,000 per month! Firms use three major methods to determine housing allowances.

The first method involves a flat allowance. In this case the employee is given a fixed amount (often depending on family size and organizational rank) to spend on housing. If the employee finds something suitable for less than the allowance, he or she can pocket the difference. If suitable housing is more than the allowance, the difference comes from the employee's pocket. This method works fine if firms have accurate, up-to-date knowledge of the housing market in the country of assignment.

The second method is to determine the housing costs of employees in their country of origin and the cost of housing in the country of assignment. If the housing costs in the country of assignment are higher, an allowance equal to that difference is paid.

In the third method, the firm provides housing in the country of assignment either rent-free or at the same cost it would be back in the employee's country of origin. Most firms that provide housing rather than a money allowance charge employees rental fees similar to those they would pay in their country of origin.

Utilities Allowances

There are two general approaches to how utility allowances are handled. The first approach is to simply provide a utility allowance to the employee. Similar to set housing allowances, firms must have an accurate knowledge of utility rates and reasonable usage in the country of assignment. The costs of overpaying for utilities or not allowing enough to, say, run an air conditioner in hot, tropical climates can be equally high. The second method is to assess the cost differentials between the country of assignment and origin and provide a utility allowance equal to the difference if utility costs are higher in the country of assignment.

Furnishing Allowances

Firms handle furnishing allowances in three major ways. The first involves shipping the employee's furnishings to the new location. There is usually a maximum weight limit, such as 15,000 pounds (roughly 6,800 kilos), set on what can be shipped. The benefit of this approach is that you would have your own furniture and home furnishings. The downside is that you may experience both damage and delays.

Consequently, many firms either purchase or, more often, lease household furnishings and then provide them free to international managers. This approach is often accompanied by a shipment of less than 1,000 pounds of personal belongings. In this case, firms sometimes pay for the storage of furniture during the assignment. While this may seem to be a simple task, be careful and make sure your household goods are properly stored. Otherwise, you may find yourself sharing a sentiment similar to the following one we recently encountered: "Almost all of our personal effects were ruined while in storage. It was difficult and extremely stressful to straighten the mess out."

The third approach is simply to provide the employee with a fixed sum of money (say $8,000-$10,000) with which furnishings can be purchased. Often, if desired furnishings cost less than the set amount, the employee is free to keep the difference; if they cost more, the employee must cover the difference.

Education Allowances

Children's education is a critical issue in the minds of most parents who are asked to transfer to a foreign country. So in countries where local school quality is not acceptable or where children would have an unreasonably difficult time adjusting to the school and local language, most firms provide an education allowance that covers the normal education costs (tuition, books, supplies, etc.) of attending local "international" schools.   If adequate education facilities are not available in the country of assignment, many firms provide assistance that covers part of the cost of boarding schools back in the country of origin. Sometimes this will even include allowances for one or two round-trip tickets for the children to visit the parents. In the more limited allowances, only airfare is provided, without boarding-school support or assistance.

Home Leave Allowances

Most companies provide airfare between the country of assignment and origin once a year for executive employees and their families. Employees sometimes prefer being given the equivalent sum in cash to use as they please. This allows them to take their home leave away from home by visiting some other place or country, or to select an inexpensive plan that allows them to do both. However, as we will discuss in chapter eight, you should seriously consider taking at least part of your home leave in your home country.

Relocation Allowances

The relocation allowance is provided in recognition that a variety of expenses are incurred that cannot be accurately predicted and whose content varies by individual. These miscellaneous expenses associated with the move are typically covered by a fixed allowance equal to one month's salary or $5,000—whichever is less. Almost half of all European and U.S. firms pay a flat sum at the beginning and end of the assignment.

Rest and Relaxation Allowances

Rest and relaxation (R&R) allowances are most often associated with hardship assignments. Generally they are provided in order for the employee and family to get away and recover from the hardships of the country of assignment. These trips are often necessary in order to purchase goods or receive medical care not available in the country. Many firms have a "use it or lose it" policy with R&R allowances because they do not want employees or their families to make the trade-off of risking physical or emotional health for the allowance money.

Medical

Because the health of employees or their families is not something that firms can afford to put at risk, most firms pay for all medical expenses (often excluding optical and dental). Some firms prefer to pay for those medical expenses in excess of what is covered by insurance. In developing countries this can mean that the firm pays for employees or members of their families to receive adequate medical care in countries other than the country of assignment.

Car and Driver Allowances

Except for senior executives, most firms provide a car allowance based on the differential of owning and operating a car in the country of assignment compared to the country of origin. External market pressures seem to be the biggest determinants of whether a car or a car and driver are provided to senior executives.

Club Membership Allowances

In some countries, club memberships are the only, or least expensive, means of the employee and family gaining access to safe recreational facilities such as tennis, swimming, exercise rooms, and so on. This type of allowance is usually reserved for senior managers or for countries in which access to safe recreational activities is quite limited.

CURRENT TRENDS

Now that we have reviewed most major components of international assignment compensation, let us elaborate a bit more on current trends. As we mentioned, just because we covered this approach or that approach to compensation or this allowance or that allowance, we do not want to create the impression that you should expect everything we have mentioned to be a part of your package. In general, there is a significant trend to reduce the cost of expatriate compensation and limit allowances.

Leaping Ahead To The Past

Because expatriate compensation can become quite complex and expensive, increasingly policy makers are saying, "Give these managers an extra 20% and send them." Interestingly, these changes in expatriate compensation actually represent a return to the past. In the early days of expatriate compensation, say in the 1950s, most managers were given a little extra, and off they went.

This approach is becoming quite common for young managers sent on development assignments. If you are young (in your 20s or early 30s), the best way to miss out on an international assignment opportunity is to get too caught up in asking for every allowance under the sun. Our advice to you, especially if you are single, is to be comfortable that you will not starve in the target country; take the assignment and make the best of it. The career payoff for a successful experience will come soon enough.

A Broader Perspective

As we mentioned at the beginning of this chapter, focusing solely on money only serves to distort the overall value of an international assignment. Clearly, adequate financial compensation has to be there to entice you to go; however, we encourage you to take a broader perspective. Keep in mind that if expatriate costs continue to climb, many companies will reduce them by reducing the number of assignments. For example, we know one company that estimated its incremental expatriate costs at $80 million for 500 expatriates. It cut this cost in half by simply reducing the number of expatriates in half. This is important to you, because as international experience increasingly becomes a necessary part of your career history in order to reach positions of significant responsibility, and if international assignment opportunities are reduced, so are your opportunities for career development and even advancement.

Trends Relative to Allowances

As we mentioned, there is a general trend toward reducing allowances. Still, we want to mention some specific trends.

Foreign service premium. The first allowance to consider is the foreign service premium allowance. As international assignments become expected experiences for advancement to senior management positions, companies quickly drop this allowance.

Hardship allowances. While firms in the past may have paid hardship allowances of $1000 to $5000 for cities such as Hong Kong, Seoul, Singapore, Taipei, and Tokyo, those days are basically gone. Today, hardship allowances are generally paid only for *very* unsafe, remote, or harsh locales.

Housing allowance. Increasingly, firms are unwilling to pay for "housing equalization." If you have a five-member family, you will probably be unwilling to move them into a two-bedroom apartment in Tokyo. However, it is unlikely that you can expect to be given an allowance that would allow you to live in a 3,000-square-foot home, such as the one you had in the suburbs of Chicago—a $350,000 annual expense for such a home in Tokyo. And Tokyo is only one of dozens of cities in which equivalent housing is so prohibitively expensive that it is basically unrealistic to expect an allowance that would provide for housing equalization.

Furnishing allowance. In moves of any significant distance, companies are increasingly providing a lump sum for furnishings and an allowance for shipping less than 1000 pounds of personal items, rather than shipping all your belongings and furniture.

Home leave. Increasingly, and with good reason, companies are requiring employees to spend at least some of their home-leave time in their home country. Although we will discuss this in more detail in chapter eight, much of the rationale is aimed at facilitating a successful repatriation.

Relocation allowances. In the past, some firms have provided annual relocation allowances to cover unexpected expenses associated with international assignments. Those days are gone. Today, if a relocation allowance is provided, it is typically given at the beginning and end of the assignment.

SUMMARY

An international assignment is a great personal and career opportunity. Money is both an important factor to you and your company. However, as we have stressed throughout this chapter, you need to consider both financial and nonfinancial benefits of the assignment. In terms of the financial compensation, both you and your firm face an internal market. Your firm must offer enough financial compensation to attract quality candidates and structure its policy so that employees feel they have been treated fairly. On the other hand, you have your own personal needs and values. You will naturally want compensation that meets those needs. However, keep in mind that in most cases you are not the only qualified candidate for a particular position. Take care not to "price yourself out of the market."

But above all this, in your discussions of financial compensation with your firm take a problem-solving approach. Do not make the discussions adversarial. Try to understand the rationale behind the particular policies or practices of your firm. Help its managers understand your specific concerns and needs. When this approach is used, we have seen dozens of cases in which creative and innovative solutions were created that met the needs of both the firm and the expatriate.

Chapter Five

What Do I Need To Know?

If you've read this far, you are no doubt convinced of the folly of thinking that an international assignment is like any other transfer, or that a great domestic track record will guarantee success overseas. The question now becomes, "What do I need to know to increase my chances of success of adjusting to and performing well in my international assignment?" The answer to this question begins with an understanding of what cross-cultural adjustment is and why it is so difficult. Once you understand the dynamics of cross-cultural adjustment, it is much easier to understand what preparation and knowledge you need in order to triumph.

UNDERSTANDING CULTURE

What is it that can make effective cross-cultural adjustment so difficult for managers and their families? Why do people who seem to have adjusted to and succeeded in a variety of situations back home sometimes struggle with adjusting to living and working in a foreign country? Without getting too philosophical, we first need to examine the question "What is culture?"

Culture as a Tree

Culture is a word we use all the time. How would you define culture? People often think about culture as though it is something a country or region has, something you can see, hear, touch, smell, or taste. People point to architecture, ceremonies, clothing, historical landmarks, art, and food as examples of a country's culture. Clearly, these things differ substantially from one country to another. The interesting question, however, is *why?*

To understand why these things vary from country to country, we first need an overall picture of culture. One approach is to think about culture is as a tree. The leaves of the tree consist of those things we can easily see and are fun to compare—visible aspects of the culture such as clothing, customs, food, etc. However, this is only a small portion of what the culture really is. Still, most people focus on these visible elements, precisely because they are easy to see. Many training programs also focus on these elements. Those types of programs tend to take a "do's and don'ts" approach to your training. They lay out a laundry list of do's and don'ts, such as don't offer a gift with your left hand in Saudi Arabia, or when negotiating in Japan don't assume that "yes" means yes; "yes" may mean no.

Culture as a Tree

**Things
We
See**

Hidden Values and Assumptions

But if customs and such do differ from one country to another, what's the problem with lists of do's and don'ts? There are two main problems. The first is that it would take an endless list of do's and don'ts to cover all the daily situations you are likely to encounter in a given foreign country over a typical three-year assignment. Second, if you created such a list, you would find all sorts of inconsistencies, because in each and every country and culture there are exceptions to the rules. So now you would need another endless list of all the exceptions. For example, when negotiating in Japan, "yes" doesn't necessarily mean yes; it may mean no, except when it means yes. If you don't understand the real roots of the cultural tree, you have no hope of coping with the thousands of specific do's and don'ts.

What lies below the surface are the values and assumptions of the culture. Like a tree, the roots that support what you see lie below the surface. So any cross-cultural adjustment requires digging below the surface and getting some understanding of the cultural value drivers and assumptions.

Culture consists of a common set of assumptions and values that consistently influence behavior, and are passed on from older to younger members of the group. The key here is that assumptions and values become part of the culture only if they are passed on from older to younger members and then reinforced. But this raises the question "What determines whether a certain value or assumption will get passed on and become a strong element of the culture?"

Quite simply, things that work get passed on. Values and assumptions that have proven successful in dealing with common challenges of life are those that get passed on, and they become a fundamental part of the culture.

They remain a part of the culture as long as they
to work. However, for values and assumptions that ..
worked for a long time, cultural inertia is difficult to
overcome — even when time-tested values and assumptions
begin to fail. Most fundamental cultural values change
through evolution rather than revolution.

If you stop and think about it, it is interesting that the
fundamental process of creating and sustaining cultural
values is the same across all cultures, and yet the specific
cultural values are different from one culture to the next.
For example, some societies, such as Canada, Australia, and
the United States, place much more importance on the
individual, while other societies, such as Japan, Pakistan,
and Columbia, place much more emphasis on the group.
For values and assumptions to become a part of the societal
fabric, they must be passed on from one generation to
another. In all societies, the values and assumptions that
work get passed on. Yet as mentioned, societies hold
different values and assumptions about the same major
challenges in life. Recognition of this fact leads to an
important conclusion: *There are multiple ways of successfully
dealing with life's challenges.*

This is perhaps one of the most important things people
who are successful in adjusting to living and working in a
foreign culture recognize. This does not mean that you
have to accept a foreign culture's behaviors, values, or
assumptions as "right," or that you must adopt them as
your own; however, it does mean that you need to
recognize that the only reason your values are different
from theirs is because a different set of values and
assumptions proved more successful in your culture than in
theirs. But their cultural values and assumptions were
successful enough to be passed on from one generation to
another.

This fact should inspire respect from us for any culture. Just think about how arrogant and ethnocentric the opposite perspective sounds. "Yes, I know a whole society has tested these values and assumptions over time and has proven them to be successful at meeting life's challenges — successful enough to be judged worthy of passing them on from one generation to another — but I happen to think they are stupid and inferior." So while we do not have to accept or adopt other cultures, when you think that their cultural values exist because they have proven successful, it is hard not to at least respect them.

You can add to this perspective a much more practical reason for having a respectful attitude toward other cultures. To illustrate this point, all you have to do is think of culture as mental road maps and traffic signals. The road maps tell you what the important and valued goals are, and what highways or lowways can get you where you want to go. The traffic rules tell you who has the right-of-way, when to stop, how to signal a left turn, when U-turns are allowed, and so on. Imagine being put in the middle of the heart of New Delhi without a map, no road signs, and no idea of the rules regarding speed limits, changing lanes, following distance, or even which side of the road to drive on. Self-preservation says we ought to respect other cultures and their traffic rules.

If you think of culture as road maps and traffic signals, going overseas without taking advantage of advanced training or educating ourselves is a scary thought. Once you realize that the road maps and traffic rules that worked for you in the past could get you lost, or in the worst case set you up for a head-on collision, preparation and training take on a new level of importance.

Cultural Values That Matter

However, just as the violation of some traffic rules is accompanied by simple warnings or small fines, and other violations are accompanied by jail time, not all rules of a culture have equal punishments or rewards attached to them, and therefore are not equally important to understand. A helpful way to think about this is to conceptualize the rules on two dimensions — the extent to which they are *widely shared* among group members and the extent to which they are *deeply held*. This conceptualization is illustrated below.

Matrix of Cultural Strength

		Breadth of Values	
		Narrow	**Wide**
Depth of Values	**Shallow**	Values shared by a narrow segment of the society. Values held at a shallow level. These values are not fundamental to the society Small impact on daily behavior. Violation of these values leads to mild and inconsistent consequences.	Values shared by most people of the society. Values held at a shallow level. These values are not fundamental to the society. Medium impact on daily behavior. Violation of these values leads to mild but consistent consequences.
	Deep	Values shared by a narrow segment of the society. Values held at a deep level. These values are fundamental to a segment of the society (i.e., subculture). Strong impact on daily behavior. Violation of these values leads to strong and consistent consequences.	Values shared by most people of the society. Values held at a deep level. These values are fundamental to the whole society. Strong impact on daily behavior. Violation of these values leads to strong and consistent consequences.

Those assumptions, values, or rules of the culture which are widely shared and deeply held generally have substantial rewards or punishments attached to them. For example, one widely shared and strongly held rule in Sweden or the U.S. (one that might even surprise you) is that you do not talk to yourself constantly or loudly. When others see a person doing this, they become nervous and concerned, even if the person poses no physical threat to anyone. After all, it isn't "normal." What happens to those who violate this rule? They often get locked up in mental institutions.

What about values that are deeply held but not widely shared? In this case, the rewards and punishments are consistent within the subculture that holds those values. For example, burping after a meal is considered by some to be a serious violation of proper behavior, but not by all. You will not be put in jail for burping. However, you would be cut out of particular social circles. In other countries, a very effective way to offend a host is by *not* burping after a meal.

In the case of widely shared but not deeply held rules, violations of the rules often carry with them uniform but rather mild punishments. In many cases, infrequent violation of these rules may carry no punishment at all. For example, not interrupting someone when they are talking to you is a generally accepted rule of good conduct in the U.S. However, if one occasionally interrupts, it is unlikely that this behavior will be accompanied by any significant punishment.

Given this simplified conceptualization, it is easy to see that the most important cultural values to learn are those that are widely shared and deeply held. These values have a strong impact on the daily behavior of people.

But how can you begin to figure out and then learn about those values? The answer to this question lies in the essence of how values become widely shared and deeply held. As we mentioned, for values to be widely shared they need to be passed on. Think about the values you hold deeply. Who taught them to you? When did you learn them? No doubt you learned many of the values you hold today from your parents when you were quite young. Because you were young, impressionable, and trusting of your parents, many of the values they taught you likely became deeply ingrained.

Now take a minute and think about how your parents taught you those values. One of the most common ways is through stories—children's stories. At a superficial level, children's stories are just that. But at a deeper level, these stories are all about the culture of the society. Almost all children's stories have a moral. Think about it for a moment. What is the moral of the story for Daniel Boone, Paul Bunyon, or Davy Crocket? Don't these stories all point to the values of rugged individualism? In contrast, the moral to stories like *The 47 Samurai* in Japan focuses on the importance of a group or collective. Maybe stories such as these in the U.S. or Japan have multiple morals to them, but they all communicate values beyond the facts of the stories. This leads us to our first practical preparation strategy: To learn the values of a particular culture quickly, read the most popular children's stories of that culture.

It may seem like a simple strategy, but it works like a charm. Not only do children's stories reveal core cultural values, but they become a way to strike up a conversation with virtually anyone from that culture. Mention that you were reading such and such story and ask them to explain the moral or significance of the story. Most people love to explain their own culture to someone who seems genuinely interested.

Assumptions that Make a Practical Difference

If we return to our cultural tree metaphor, you will recall that below behaviors and below values lie assumptions, the source from which values and behaviors flow. We tend to think that fundamental assumptions, such as those concerning the nature of the people (are they basically good and industrious, or evil and lazy?) should be the concern of philosophers. While some may think there's no practical reason for examining a culture's underlying assumptions, nothing could be further from the truth. Understanding the fundamental assumptions within a culture may be one of the most practical things you could ever know. As a manager for Lockheed Martin commented to us:

> Understanding cultural assumptions is like knowing the thrust, trajectory, and total fuel of a rocket. If you know these fundamentals, you can basically predict where the rocket is going to land. If you understand a culture's fundamental assumptions, you can basically predict where people are going to land—how they are going to behave, if their behavior can be changed, or what it might take to change it.

The underlying assumptions of almost any culture can be divided into a five-part categorization. The figure on the next page provides a summary of the general nature of these assumptions and examples of the specific forms they might take, as well as their management implications. After we briefly examine the basic types of assumptions and how differences can influence behavior, we will take a look at some general ways of uncovering and understanding a culture's fundamental assumptions.

BASIC ASSUMPTIONS AND THEIR IMPLICATIONS

Nature of Assumptions	Specific Assumptions	Management Implications
Environment (assumptions about the relationship between humans and the environment)	• People are meant to dominate the environment. • People must be submissive to the environment.	• Strategic plans should be developed to enable them to dominate the industry. • Firms should seek positions that allow them to coexist with others.
Human nature (assumptions about human nature)	• People are generally lazy. • Work is as natural as play for people.	• Implement procedures to monitor behavior and establish clear punishment for undesired behaviors. • Provide people with opportunities and responsibilities and encourage their development.
Relationships (assumptions about how humans should relate to each other	• Individuals have certain rights and freedoms. • People exist because of others and owe an obligation to them	• Individual performance should be measured and rewarded. • Cooperation with and contributions to the group should be rewarded.
Activity (assumptions about the proper types and targets of human activity)	• People create their own destinies and must plan for the future. • People should react to and enjoy whatever the present provides.	• People who fail to plan should plan to fail. • Planning for the future only gets in the way of enjoying the present
Truth (assumptions about the nature of truth and reality)	• Truth objectively exists. • Truth is what is socially accepted.	• Facts and statistics are presented to convince and influence people. • Opinion leaders are utilized to influence decisions.

Humanity's Relationship to the Environment

The first area of assumptions concerns those made about the relationship of humanity to nature. For example, in some cultures, the assumption is that humans are here to dominate nature and use the environment for the wealth and benefit of mankind. In other cultures, the assumption is that humans and nature are to coexist harmoniously. The practical implications of these differing assumptions can be quite significant. In the United States, the dominance assumption is an important basis for building dams, mining minerals, or logging trees. However, the implications may reach beyond these basic activities to strategic planning or management practices in business as well. Consider how most U.S. firms view their business environment and how they strategically approach it. Is the business environment viewed as something that people must accept and with which they must try to harmonize? Or is it viewed as something that must be mastered and dominated if possible? Most strategic plans in U.S. companies do not talk about coexisting harmoniously with their competitors. They talk about dominating the industry and being number one; but not every culture shares this basic assumption. The key to gaining a comprehensive understanding of the culture is to ask questions that help you get at the assumptions about this relationship.

The Nature of Human Nature

Different cultures also make different assumptions about the nature of people. Some cultures assume people are fundamentally industrious, while others assume they are inherently lazy. Douglas McGregor wrote about this in his classic management book *The Human Side of Enterprise*. McGregor argued that every manager acted on a "theory" or set of assumptions about people. Theory X managers assumed that "the average human being has an inherent dislike for work and will avoid it if he can." Consequently, managers accepting this view of people believe that "people must be coerced, controlled, directed, and threatened with punishment to get them to put forth adequate effort toward the achievement of organizational objectives." On the other hand, Theory Y managers assume that "the expenditure of physical and mental effort in work is as natural as play or rest." Consequently, managers accepting this view of people believe that "external control and the threat of punishment are not the only means for bringing about effort toward organizational objectives. Man will exercise self-direction and self-control in the service of objectives to which he is committed. Commitment to objectives is a function of the rewards associated with their achievement." To understand the deeper roots of the management style, you need to try to understand the cultural assumptions about people and their inherent nature.

The Nature of Human Relationships

This area of assumptions deals with a variety of questions: What is the right way for people to deal with each other? How much power and authority should any one person have over another? How much of individuals' orientation should be toward themselves versus others? For example, in the Philippines, Venezuela, and Mexico, people are much more accepting of hierarchical differences than in Australia, Israel, and the United States. In the former countries, fundamental assumptions hold essentially that it is right for there to be hierarchical and status differences, and that appropriate behavior of people toward each other depends on their relative status. These differences can have a significant impact on business and management practices, such as the decision-making process. In Japan, subordinates would rarely challenge decisions made by their superiors because of the underlying assumption that there should be significant power differences between superiors and subordinates. In Australia, subordinates are much more likely to openly challenge decisions made by their superiors because they assume significantly smaller power differences between superiors and subordinates. Cultures can also differ in their assumptions about the importance of the individual versus the group. In the U.S. and Australia, for example, individualism is assumed to be best. In countries such as Japan, Korea, and Pakistan, people assume that the group is most important. Discovering the fundamental assumptions of the particular culture you need to understand requires digging into and asking questions about authority, hierarchy, status, individualism, group orientation, and so on.

The Nature of Human Activity

This area of assumptions concerns issues of what is right for people to do and whether they should be active, passive, or fatalistic in these activities. In the U.S., people brag about working eighty hours a week, about having no time for vacations or watching TV, and about doing several things at the same time on their computers. They believe in phrases such as "people who fail to plan should plan to fail." In other cultures, such high-strung activity is not valued, and may even be seen as a waste of time and energy. They believe that such preoccupation with planning only gets in the way of enjoying the present. As you can see, understanding the roots of a culture requires going beyond observing the activities people do or don't engage in, and probing into how they view activity in general and what they see as the purpose.

The Nature of Reality and Truth

Different cultures also hold differing assumptions about the nature of reality and truth and how they are verified or established. For example, the adversarial criminal law system in countries such as Canada is based on the assumption that truth exists and that the light generated by opposing views will ultimately illuminate what really happened. The former CEO of ITT, Herold Geneen, always talked about "the unshakable facts," or those that would hold up even after intense scrutiny. If the underlying assumption is that truth really exists, then directly pounding away at a problem makes sense. However, other cultures assume that reality is much more subjective and dependent on what people believe it to be. Consequently, opinion leaders or persuasive stories rather than "unshakable facts" are used as means of influencing people; business decisions and problems are not attacked directly.

The Nature of Time

Different cultures also form differing assumptions about the nature of time. Is time assumed to be a river or a lake? Those that view time as a river generally hold linear assumptions about time. Like a river, time moves on in a linear fashion. What you do not take advantage of today will be gone tomorrow. This assumption creates a great emphasis on time management, being punctual for appointments, keeping appointment books, and so on. The phenomenal success of Franklin Quest (now Franklin Covey), a producer of relatively expensive day-planner systems for individuals, is testimony to this orientation in the United States. Franklin has grown at a rate several times that of the general economy for the last decade. Recently, it has moved with great success into Japan, another culture with linear assumptions about time. Those that view time as a lake generally hold nonlinear assumptions about time. Like a lake, what you do not dip from the lake today will be there for you to use tomorrow. This has nearly the opposite affect on management behaviors: being late for an appointment is not seen as a character flaw; setting specific day, hour, and minute schedules is seen as unnecessary.

Summary

Discussing these six areas of assumptions illustrates two key issues. First, as mentioned earlier, assumptions are the source from which values and behaviors flow. In order to understand the visible aspects of culture, one must understand the invisible values and assumptions. Second, fundamental assumptions by their very nature are not only invisible, but are generally taken for granted. Their taken-for-granted nature makes them difficult to uncover or understand because the people who hold them are not generally conscious of them, and therefore cannot easily identify and explain them to foreigners. They are as unaware of their cultural assumptions as they are about the oxygen in the air around them.

Furthermore, the taken-for-granted nature of cultural assumptions means they are not easily changed. This is important to understand. We have known many managers who have mistakenly interpreted a change in behavior as a fundamental change in values or assumptions. For example, Japanese discontinued wearing kimonos and started wearing Western clothes. Some may conclude from this that the Japanese have adopted Western values. To understand that a change at the surface had no effect on values and assumptions below the surface, you only need to recognize that most Japanese businessmen wear virtually the same Western business clothing—dark suit, white shirt, and conservative tie. The same assumptions about group conformity that led to everyone wearing kimonos was still alive and strong, the main driver behind everyone wearing similar business attire.

This gets to the heart of why cross-cultural adjustment is not an easy feat to achieve. First, although culture has both visible (behaviors) and invisible components (values and assumptions), the invisible components are the most important because they are the source of the visible aspects of a foreign culture. Unfortunately, most of us have neither the mental maps of the invisible terrain or the unspoken but generally understood traffic rules. Without these mental maps, it is only natural that in our travels we encounter everything from close calls to serious cultural crashes.

Chapter Six

How Do I Prepare?

At this point it should be easy to see why cross-cultural training is a must if you are to succeed overseas. If you were a professional basketball player, would you consider going into a game without adequate training and preparation? Would you want to go into a game in which you had not reviewed film on the other team and developed a game plan?

We encourage you to take advantage of any training and preparation your firm has to offer. Unfortunately, some firms do not provide cross-cultural training for their managers before sending them abroad. Often this is because executives assume that business is business and good management is good management. So if the candidate has been successful in the Hong Kong, he or she will be successful in France, Brazil or anywhere else.

But business is not business, and what makes a manager succeed in Hong Kong will not necessarily lead to success in New York or vice versa. Furthermore, well designed cross-cultural training programs can enhance your job performance, adjustment to the new culture, and development of cross-cultural managerial skills.

Designing Training

Keep in mind, however, that just as business is not generic, neither is training. Training effectiveness is a function of matching your specific situation to the required amount and level or rigor of training.

Training Rigor

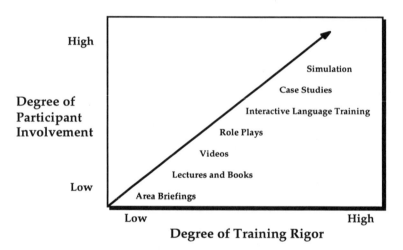

Let's talk for a minute about what we mean by *training rigor*. Training rigor is basically how much mental involvement and effort you and the trainer must expend in order for you to learn the desired content. *Low rigor training* includes approaches such as films, lectures, books and area-briefings. As an example, it doesn't take much mental involvement to sit back and watch a video on "Doing Business in China." *Medium rigor training* requires you to become more involved in the process. Typically, this involves practicing skills that you first learn by watching someone else and then repeating what you've seen. For example, most language training is done this way. The instructor first says a word or phrase, and then you repeat it. A slightly more rigorous approach to cultural skills involves (1) watching the instructor perform the task, such as properly conducting introductions during a negotiation, (2) repeating the behavior but being videotaped, and (3) then watching the video of yourself for enhanced feedback. *High-rigor approaches* require significant participant involvement and include methods such as assessment centers, interactive language training, and sophisticated cross-cultural simulations (see the Training Rigor figure). For example, one of the more sophisticated simulations we have used is called Global Tycoon™, a computer-based simulation in which individuals are put into teams. Each team runs a company, setting its strategy and making decisions from ordering raw materials to allocating advertising dollars and everything in between. Participants become very engaged in the process and learn a variety of lessons about conducting business across multiple geographic and cultural borders.

However, even if you accept that training is needed, and even if you understand that different levels of rigor might be designed into the training, a critical question remains: How rigorous should my training program be? Generally, the more rigorous the training, the more expensive it is because it requires more time and more sophisticated and highly skilled trainers. Keep in mind, however, that even though you pay for rigorous training, you also pay a price for inadequate training. If the training you receive is not rigorous enough to prepare you adequately for your assignment, you and your family will pay the consequences. On the other hand, you do not want to go "hunting quail with an elephant gun." Basically, three dimensions determine the appropriate level of training rigor: 1) cultural toughness, 2) communication toughness, and 3) job toughness.

Dimension 1: Cultural Toughness

Simply put, *Cultural Toughness* is the extent to which the underlying values and ways of doing business are different between two different cultures. If we assume that someone born and raised in the United States is being sent on an international assignment, the list on the next page provides a categorization of countries by *culture* toughness (not by standard of living) from those that are relatively tough (i.e., different) to those that are relatively easy to adjust to for Americans.

Keep in mind, however, that just because a country is listed as "less tough" does not mean adjustment will be a snap, and therefore no training is needed. While adjusting to England for an American might be easier than adjusting to China, we have worked with many managers and families who found that adjusting to a "culturally similar" country had significant challenges.

Finally, keep in mind that the list provided is for general use. Obviously, if you are being sent to Japan, and you have lived and worked there before, its "cultural toughness" will not be as high for you.

However, do not make the mistake we have seen people make in thinking that because they were familiar with the country and culture, there was little need for training for their *spouse*. You may have all the best intentions of helping a spouse or family member learn about the culture. However, our experience is that this good intention may not translate into the results you envision, for two reasons.

CULTURAL TOUGHNESS FOR AMERICANS

MOST DIFFICULT

China
South Korea
Saudi Arabia
Peru
Japan
Portugal
Brazil
Kenya
Mexico
Taiwan
Chile
Argentina
France
Italy
Hong Kong
Singapore
Sweden
Great Britain
Australia
New Zealand
Canada

LEAST DIFFICULT

First, you may find that your spouse "is not the greatest student," and your spouse may equally feel that you "are not the greatest teacher." Learning together can be a great experience, but "teaching" and "being taught" are generally more difficult for couples to do successfully. Second, you are quite likely to find that the pressures and demands of the job simply take away the time you had intended to spend helping your spouse learn about the culture.

Dimension 2: Communication Toughness

The second factor in determining the needed degree of rigor in a cross-cultural training program is the extent of expected interpersonal interaction between you and the local populace. The more you have to interact with host nationals, the higher the level of Communication Toughness. The boxed questions can help highlight the degree to which you must interact with local nationals. The level of training rigor should increase proportionately with the frequency and intensity of interactions with local constituencies such as employees, government officials, customers, and suppliers.

Communication Toughness Assessment

1. Are the rules and norms for communicating very different from those in your home country, or are they quite similar?

2. Will you have to communicate frequently or infrequently with the local workers?

3. Is English the national language? If not, how difficult is the foreign language to learn?

---

4. Will you have to communicate mainly in one direction (e.g., giving orders, delegating, giving presentations, and so on), or will the nature of the job require intensive two-way communication (e.g., consultations, hosting parties, business negotiations) with local nationals?

5. What will be the main form of communicating with local nationals? Face-to-face (intimate, daily discussions with subordinates) or technical (memos, mail, and so on)?

6. How long will you be in the position with the communication challenges that are inherent in the assignment? Six months? One year? Three years?

7. What will be the main type of interaction, formal (based on position, title, and authority) or informal (based on personal influence and developing relationships)?

8. Will you have to communicate with a narrow or broad group of constituencies (subordinates, peers, superiors, alliance partners, suppliers, customers, government officials)?

Dimension 3: Job Toughness

If you are like most people, your position overseas will be a step up in authority and autonomy, and may even involve a formal title higher than the one you held before going. This often means new issues, more responsibilities, and new challenges to face. The tougher the tasks of the new job, the more assistance you will need through rigorous training methods prior to departure. The boxed questions can help highlight the degree to which cross-cultural training could help you in your new job.

Job Toughness Assessment

1. Are the performance standards the same?
2. Is the degree of personal involvement required in the work unit the same?
3. Is the task the same or quite different?
4. Are the bureaucratic procedures that must be followed similar?
5. Are the resource limitations the same?
6. Are the legal restrictions similar?
7. Are the technological limitations familiar?
8. Is the freedom to decide how the work gets done the same?
9. Are the choices about what work gets delegated similar?
10. Is the freedom to decide who does which tasks the same?

Training Timing

Although a careful analysis of these three dimensions is necessary before valid cross-cultural training can be designed, you should also consider the timing of the training in order for it to be as effective as possible. Most training consultants only talk about, and most managers only consider, predeparture training.   Predeparture training is important, but it has its limitations. Predeparture training should focus mostly on basic, day-to-day, survival-level concerns, because you will encounter these issues as soon as they step off the plane.   As time passes in the new country, you will have less need for training concerning day-to-day survival issues. While you can benefit from learning some of the deep and profound aspects of the culture before your international assignment, you can benefit most from learning in-depth cross-cultural content *after* you are in the country.

Keep in mind that mastery of "culturally tough" concepts will *not* automatically come with time.   Certainly, you will learn about the culture just by being in it as time passes. However, remember that much of the culture lies below the surface, out of sight.   It takes deliberate digging to uncover cultural roots.   Also keep in mind that *you don't know what you don't know.* And so, it's difficult in advance to know what you need to know.   This is one reason why you'll need postarrival training to maximize your chances for success. There are several additional reasons as well.

First, you will have higher levels of motivation to learn deeper and more complicated aspects of the culture after you've been there for a couple of months. This is primarily because after you have bumped into the more subtle and important aspects of the culture and have a few bruises on your head, you'll want to avoid unnecessarily banging your head on cultural walls in the future. As an executive from IBM who participated in a postarrival program we conducted in Asia stated, "Once you've encountered the crazy way they make decisions here, it motivates you to understand why and how to deal with it. Before coming here, you couldn't have convinced me that they thought about and made decisions that differently.   Believe me. They do!"

Second, you will have more experience with the local culture that you can relate the training to. This experience will provide you with a foundation for learning deeper cultural values, norms, and ideas. As an Brazilian executive from Exxon who participated in a postarrival program in the U.S. commented, "Before coming to the U.S., I was like a coat rack without any arms. You could throw things on me, but not all of them would stick. After three months here, I had arms. Now this training program about doing business in the U.S. sticks. I've got some experience to hang [the content of the training program] on."

Third, you will be in an environment where you can immediately apply in the workplace what you learn. Nothing facilitates retention like application. During the week-long postarrival program for the IBM executives, two of the participants went out and tried things the very night they learned them to see if they worked. The effect was immediate and exactly what the trainer said it would be. This not only helped the IBM executives retain the concept, but further enhanced their motivation for the rest of the seminar.

Fourth, with postarrival training you will be in an environment that itself lends a "reality" factor to the training that cannot be had when training is undertaken in the home country prior to the assignment. For example, in a postarrival program we conducted in Japan, one of the key cultural concepts involved the notion of *Giri*, or duty and obligation. This lesson is taught to all Japanese when they are children through the true story of the 47 Samurai. It is one thing to tell the story to a group of Americans on assignment in Japan; it is quite another to visit the temple where these samurai are buried and watch people come pay their respects by lighting incense and offering prayers.

Training Timing

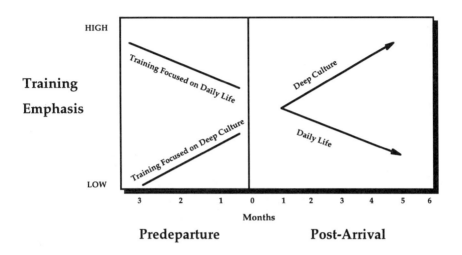

In terms of timing, most predeparture training should finish a month before departure, and in-country training should not really begin until two to four weeks after arrival in the country. Predeparture training should finish a month before you leave because you and your family will be overwhelmed with all the logistics of the move and have little energy or attention to focus on retaining knowledge from the training programs. Postarrival training should not begin until about a month after you have arrived for exactly the same reason. It will take you a few weeks just to get settled in to the point that you can really concentrate on the content of a training program. However, postarrival training should occur before you have been in the country six or seven months. Postarrival training after that point is not going to be very effective. The reason is simple. It is nearly impossible to suspend judgment for six months. It is human nature to form judgments and come to conclusions. The problem is that most of us do not change our conclusions once they are formed, even if we are wrong. Postarrival training, therefore, should not occur before you've had some time to settle in and experience living and working in the culture, but it should happen before you've come to your own conclusions about the culture.

Training Content

Hopefully, at this point you now have a clearer idea of why you can benefit from training and education both before and after you arrive in the host country, and a clearer idea of how rigorous the training and education should be. The next logical question is what content should go into that education effort? To some extent, we have already answered this question. To the extent that cross-cultural adjustment is important to your success overseas, the host country culture should be an important part of any educational effort you undertake. Furthermore, if culture consists of visible aspects such as food and customs, as well as invisible aspects such as values and fundamental assumptions, then these general topics need to be included somewhere within the total education effort. However, we can offer even more detailed content advice than this.

Quite simply, you need to learn what people in that culture learn. Remember, cultural values are learned at an early age. The most influential aspects of the culture are reinforced throughout a person's life in that culture from various angles. For most cultures this means understanding families, education, religion, and work. The following are some introductory questions to address in starting your study of the culture:

General Cultural Questions

Family

1. Do extended family members live together?

2. Are family leadership responsibilities shared or strictly divided by gender?

3. How different are the gender roles that boys and girls learn?

Education

1. Does education stress rote learning or problem solving?

2. Is education centrally-controlled or managed at the community level?

Religion

1. Is there a dominant religion in the culture?

2. How close are the ties between religious and national holidays?

Work

1. Do people live to work or work to live?

2. Is status more a function of what one does, who one works for, or who one is by virtue of birth?

The sample questions provided are just that. Literally dozens of questions on each topic would need to be addressed in order to gain a deep understanding of the culture. Each topic will require significant time and energy to understand.

However, a comprehensive understanding of the culture will require one more step. It will require linking these various topics together. Even though these topics can and often do need to be studied separately, individuals in that culture experience work, family, religion, or education in an intertwined and interactive fashion. Consequently, not only do you need to understand each of the topics in their own right, but you need to understand how they reinforce each other, oppose each other, or balance each other in order to fully appreciate how they affect people's thinking, feelings, and behavior.

Furthermore, there is a tendency to examine these issues at "maturity," that is, from an adult perspective. For example, when examining the education system in a country, there is a tendency to examine it from the perspective of someone looking back who has gone through the education system of that country. People do not experience a country's educational system in its entirety. They experience kindergarten when they are young and college when they are older. It is important to keep in mind that people *grow* and *develop* in a society. Therefore, education looks very different to a five-year-old in France than to a twenty-year-old. How things look at twenty may in part be a function of how things looked at five. Thus it is important to place topics such as education, religion, family, and work in context. To do, this take advantage of every opportunity to talk with "non-adults." Children and young adults of all ages can provide cultural insights and perspectives that adults cannot. If you don't get many opportunities to talk with youngsters, ask an adult friend or acquaintance to walk through the key elements of what it was like to grow up in that country and culture. This will help you see the connections between topics, and to see each topic at different developmental and growth stages. After this overarching frame is provided, then education, religion, family, and work can be examined separately in greater depth with less distortion in the translation.

The following table provides a list of important general topics as well as key subtopics to include in a training program.

PROGRAM CONTENT

Education

   Elementary School

   Middle School

   High School

   College

Family

   Typical Parental Roles

   Discipline

   Extended Family Relations

Politics and Government

   Form of Government

   Key Political Leaders

   Role of Government in Business

Religion

   Dominant Organized Religions

   Important Holidays and Customs

Work

> Organizational and Financial Structure
>
> Decision Making
>
> Conflict Resolution
>
> Negotiation
>
> Human Resource Management

Training Programs

While most companies have internal people to cover company policies concerning housing, moving, and other logistics, they typically do not have the expert resources to provide training for international assignments. As a consequence, you will likely need to attend a program provided by an outside vendor.

Your firm may not have a history of offering any sort of training for an international assignment. Less than half of U.S. firms offer this sort of training to their international assignees. However, most human resource executives recognize the need for cross-cultural training and will likely do what they can to support your educational efforts. Even if your firm doesn't have a history of providing cross-cultural training, you may want to discuss the issue with someone. Sometimes, even if you do most of the education on your own, your firm may be willing to provide financial support for the educational materials you purchase, such as books or videos on the country and culture. If you frame your need for training in terms of setting yourself up for success, maximizing your performance, and giving the firm the best possible return on its investment in you and this assignment, company executives are likely to provide some support for your predeparture and postarrival educational efforts.

If your firm does provide support for training programs, you can enhance the effectiveness of the program by doing the following:

- Assess the cultural, communication, and job toughness of your upcoming assignment.

- Make sure that the rigor of the program matches the toughness of your assignment.

- To the extent needed and possible, take advantage of opportunities for some "in-country" follow-up training. If your company allows for postarrival language training, you may want to get language training that includes cultural issues as part of the program design.

- If you have a spouse or significant other, do everything you can to involve that person in your education effort. It is almost impossible to overemphasize the importance of spouse adjustment in the overall success of the assignment.

- If you have children, especially if they are thirteen or older, do everything you can to get them involved in the education effort.

If you have some influence on the choice of the training provider, you will want to do the five things mentioned above, plus consider the following in selecting a training provider:

- Make sure that the provider is capable of delivering both general cross-cultural adjustment and country- and culture-specific content. Dozens of providers can deliver reasonable programs on the general aspects of cross-cultural adjustment, communication, management, and so on. However, only a handful of companies have the resources and experience to provide high-quality general *and* country-specific training.

- Make sure the provider is capable of and has a history of providing programs designed for spouses and children. Although some of the needs and issues are common for all family members, spouses and children both face unique issues. In addition, children, especially younger children, learn differently than adults, and as a consequence, it is important to make sure that the provider is capable of delivering content and methods that matches their needs.

- Make sure the provider has a good understanding of the position, responsibilities, and objectives of the international assignment and can customize the content of the program to fit your needs.

CONCLUSION

In conclusion, keep several things in mind as you think about what you need to know in preparation for living and working in a foreign country and culture:

- Take advantage of every opportunity, both predeparture and postarrival, for training and education concerning the country, culture, and business environment.

- Remember that regardless of past domestic track record, most people have cross-cultural adjustment difficulties.

- These difficulties arise partly from the fact that most of the overall culture, and certainly the most important aspects of culture, lie below the surface.

- Understanding a culture can be a life-long process, so you might try to start with those aspects of the culture that are widely shared and deeply held.

- Look to children's stories to get an idea of what fundamental values are taught in that culture.

- Recognize that fundamental aspects of a culture are there because they have proven successful enough to be passed on and reinforced. That alone commands respect, but doesn't require agreement or adoption.

- Understanding fundamental cultural assumptions is practical and necessary. In general you should examine six categories of these assumptions.

- If your firm offers training, take advantage of it and incorporate it into an overall education plan. If your firm doesn't offer it, be that much more serious in creating and executing your own educational plan.

- Make sure the training rigor matches your needs.

- To the extent possible, focus your postarrival educational efforts on the deeper cultural aspects of the country.

- Make sure your educational plan covers a wide spectrum of issues so that you have a good overall understanding of cultural values and systems and how they fit together in the society.

- If you have the opportunity, take care in selecting a training provider and make sure that capabilities more than price drive the provider selection decision.

Education is not a panacea and will not guarantee your success, and training programs, while valuable and important to take advantage of, are no substitute for a personal educational plan. If the assignment is not right for you, all the education in the world may not overcome the mismatch, but if the assignment is right, few things will enhance the probability of your succeeding in the assignment more than a comprehensive educational plan that begins before you leave and continues well after you arrive in the assignment.

Chapter Seven

How Do I Facilitate Successful Adjustment?

No doubt you've heard the term *culture shock*. Even though we've all heard the term, it's interesting to see what people think it means. The following are some of the responses we've been given when we've asked people to define culture shock:

- It's the shock you feel when you see something revolting or disgusting in the culture.

- It's that thing that hits you when you encounter strange smells and odors in a new country.

- Culture shock is that feeling like "They do *that* in this country?"

- It's that surprised feeling you get when you encounter something new in the culture.

- Culture shock is a feeling of frustration with the crazy way things get done in that country.

- It's what you feel when the honeymoon is over and you realize you're going to be living in that country for several more years and you're not that thrilled.

These statements are not quite right, but they're not entirely wrong either. Perhaps the best way to zero in on what culture shock is and ways we can better cope with it is to examine a real case of a family (with disguised name) that recently experienced culture shock.

FRED BAILEY: AN INNOCENT ABROAD

Fred gazed out the window of his twenty-fourth floor office at the tranquil beauty of the Imperial Palace amidst the hustle and bustle of downtown Tokyo. It had only been six months since Fred had arrived with his wife and two children for this three-year assignment as the director of Kline & Associates' Tokyo office. Kline & Associates was a large multinational consulting firm with offices in nine countries worldwide. Fred was now trying to decide if he should simply pack up and tell the home office he was coming home, or try to somehow convince his wife and himself that they should stay and finish the assignment. Given how excited Fred thought they all were about the assignment to begin with, it was a mystery to him as to how things had gotten to this point. As he watched the swans glide across the water in the moat that surrounds the Imperial Palace, Fred reflected back on the past seven months.

Seven months ago, the managing partner of the main office in Boston, Dave Steiner, asked Fred to lunch to discuss "business." To Fred's surprise, the "business" was not the major project that he and his team had just finished, but was instead a very big promotion and career move. Fred was offered the position of managing director of the firm's relatively new Tokyo office, which had a staff of forty, including seven Americans. Most of the Americans in the Tokyo office were either associate consultants or research analysts. Fred would be in charge of the whole office and would report to a senior partner who was over the Asian region. It was implied to Fred that if this assignment went as well as his past one, it would be the last step before becoming a partner in the firm.

When Fred told his wife about the unbelievable opportunity, he was shocked at her less-than-enthusiastic response. His wife, Jenny, thought it would be rather difficult to have the children live and go to school in a foreign country for three years, especially when Christine, the oldest, would be starting middle school next year. Besides, now that the kids were in school, Jenny was thinking about going back to work--at least part-time. Jenny had a degree in fashion merchandising from a well-known private university and had worked as an assistant buyer for a large women's clothing store before having the two girls.

Fred explained that the career opportunity was just too good to pass up and that the company overseas package would making living in Japan terrific. The company would pay all the expenses to move whatever the Baileys wanted to take with them. The company had a very nice house in an expensive district of Tokyo that would be provided rent free. Additionally, the company would rent their house in Boston during their absence. Also, the firm would provide a car and driver, education expenses for the children to attend private schools, and a cost-of-living adjustment and overseas compensation that would nearly double Fred's gross annual salary. After two days of consideration and discussion, Fred told Mr. Steiner he would accept the assignment.

The current Tokyo office managing director was a partner in the firm, but had been in the new Tokyo office for less than a year when he was transferred to head up a long-established office in England. Because the transfer to England was taking place "right away," Fred and his family had about three weeks to prepare for the move. Between getting things at the office transferred to Bob Newcome, who was being promoted to Fred's position, and the logistical hassles of getting furniture and the like ready to be moved, neither Fred nor his family had much time to really find out much about Japan, other than what was in the encyclopedia.

When the Baileys arrived, they were greeted at the airport by one of the young Japanese associate consultants and the senior American expatriate. Fred and his family were quite tired from the long trip, and the two-hour ride back to Tokyo was a rather quiet one.

The first few weeks in Japan were hectic. It took the Baileys some time just to get settled into their new house. Actually it wasn't really a house but a luxury apartment. By Japanese standards it was enormous, but it was small compared to the large Colonial the Baileys left back in Boston. It was a good thing they had decided to rent their house back home, because the furniture would have overpowered their new apartment. Although Jenny missed their home, her initial reaction to the apartment was positive. It was tastefully decorated and adequate in size, and was centrally located in Hiro (an affluent neighborhood near downtown Tokyo).

Once the jet lag wore off, the Baileys got busy settling in. They found a grocery store (National Azabu) near them that carried a variety of American food products, and there was even a Baskin Robbins next to it and a Mrs. Field's Cookies down the street. During these early days, Fred used the company car and driver that had been assigned to him to shuttle the family around as they shopped, registered the girls for school, and registered at the city offices. It seemed like the first month was gone before they knew it.

After the first month or so, however, things seemed to get progressively worse. Fred got irritated just remembering some of the specific and general problems and incidents. He remembered the time his wife called him crying after getting lost on the subway; the time he bought what he had thought were pickles, but they tasted like spoiled vinegar; the time he asked a Japanese employee to prepare an important report and found out the day before it was due that it wasn't ready and that the employee didn't think it would be from the moment he had accepted the assignment; the time he stuck his chopsticks in his bowl of rice to keep them from rolling off onto the floor at an important dinner, only to be told later that doing so was a sign of death; the many times he had asked Japanese clients simple direct questions, only to receive vague responses; the increasingly frequent times he and Jenny had fought over things they never fought over back home.

And last night Jenny had dropped a bombshell. She told Fred that she was going home, and yesterday wasn't soon enough. She was sick of the country, tired of being stared at, and irritated by constantly feeling like an outsider and unable to make any Japanese friends. Fred had his own irritations with the Japanese people and country, but going home now might very well be a significant career-limiting move (CLM). On the other hand, Jenny seemed very serious.   To some extent, Jenny was forcing a choice between his marriage and his career.   The more Fred thought about the whole thing, the more frustration, anger, and anxiety built up inside.   To Fred, and especially to Jenny, the only life preserver (and perhaps marriage preserver) seemed to be to pack up and head home.

CROSS-CULTURAL ADJUSTMENT: THE PROCESS

The preceding case is both true and common.   You (or your family) should not be surprised if you experience adjustment difficulties similar to those of the Baileys. Unfortunately, while the term "culture shock" is recognized by most, its underlying process is understood by very few. This chapter describes the dynamics of cross-cultural adjustment and explains how you can deal effectively with it.

The Role of Routines

To understand culture shock, we first need to understand the role that routines, ego, and self-image play in our normal, "unshocked" lives.   Let's start by examining routines. All of us have a wide variety of routines. We not only have them, we try to establish them. Why? Partly it's because we prefer to do things a certain way or on a particular schedule.   But that's not the major reason for establishing routines.   We establish routines because we like the predictability they bring. We know what we'll do, how we'll do it, and what the consequences are likely to be.

The global success of McDonald's is testimony to the general human need for predictability. When customers go to McDonald's, they know what a Big Mac is going to taste like before they order it. The taste does not vary much by the day of the week, different locations within a given country, or even across countries. A Big Mac is a Big Mac. People not only like the product, but they like its predictability.

Routines affect all aspects of our lives, from the mundane to the critical.   For example, we establish routines concerning what we do when we wake up in the morning-- smash the alarm into pieces, get up, take a shower, get dressed, eat, run out the door, buy a new alarm clock. But we also establish more serious routines, such as how we form or develop relationships, how we deal with conflict in those relationships, and what we expect from relationships. For example, some of us establish relationships slowly and deal with problems directly, while others establish relationships quickly and deal with problems more indirectly.

As mentioned, the first and most obvious function that routines serve is in providing a level of predictability and certainty in our lives.   Our minds cannot consciously process an infinite number of issues simultaneously. Routines and the certainty they provide create a "psychological economy," if you will. Because you know what a Big Mac will taste like or because you know that once you get up you will take a shower, you do not have to devote a lot of mental time and energy to thinking about those issues or worrying about their outcomes or consequences.

When routines are disrupted, we have to devote more mental time and energy processing new issues and wondering and worrying about their consequences. To the extent that mental time and energy are limited, the disruption of routines means that we now have less mental time and energy for other things. But all disruptions are not created equal. The severity is a function of three dimensions.

Number of Disrupted Routines

The first dimension is the total number of routines that are disrupted. All other things being equal, the greater the number of routines disrupted, the more difficult it is to deal with the disruptions, and the greater the level of frustration, anger, and anxiety that are likely to follow. For example, it is one thing to have your morning shower routine disrupted, but it is quite another to have your eating, sleeping, commuting, and working routines all altered by a new cultural environment. Or it may be an inconvenience to have to give up the strong handshake for a bow in greeting someone, but it can be quite upsetting to have to alter most of the dimensions of how you delegate authority, make decisions, influence people, plan and organize your work day, and motivate your subordinates.

Degree Routines are Disrupted

The second dimension is the degree or extent of the disruption, ranging from a slight alteration to the total and complete destruction of a routine. The greater the extent of the disruption, the greater the time and energy required to deal with it, and the greater the level of associated frustration, anger, and anxiety. For example, if a shower was the first order of the day previously, having to take a bath would be somewhat of a lesser disruption compared to not being able to do either without going down the street to a public bath house. Or it may be somewhat irritating to have to switch from cash bonuses to days off as motivation incentives, but it can be totally frustrating to have your ability to administer rewards and punishments as tools of motivation completely removed from your hands and placed in those of a labor ministry.

Importance of the Disrupted Routines

The third dimension is the importance of the disrupted routine. As mentioned, not all routines are equal in importance. Some are critical, others trivial. The greater the importance of the routine disrupted, the greater the time and energy required to deal with it, and the greater the level of frustration, anger, and anxiety associated with the disruption. For example, not having the reserved parking spot you are used to is probably not as frustrating as having to change your leadership style from a "jointly discuss and then you decide" to a "total consensus" decision-making approach.

The Importance of Identity

Up to this point, the primary explanation for culture shock has been that new and unfamiliar environments of foreign cultures disrupt routines, and that (1) the more routines that are disrupted, (2) the more severely any given routine is altered, and (3) the more the disrupted routines are critical ones, the greater the time and mental energy required to cope and the greater the feelings of frustration, anger, and anxiety associated with culture shock. Despite the importance of the dynamics already described, they do not completely explain why culture shock and feelings of frustration, anger, and anxiety can be so severe.

Isaac Newton claimed that for every action there is an equal and opposite reaction. If this is true, then logically you would also expect the reverse to be true. That is, for every reaction, there is an equal and opposite cause. In terms of culture shock, you would expect that for every level and severity of culture shock, there is an equally powerful cause. Understanding the cause of severe culture shock is important because extreme levels of culture shock do occur and can be mentally and physically dangerous.

For example, Fred Bailey, at six months into his assignment in Japan, found himself frequently so angry that he had to work hard not to vent his anger by striking someone, and at other times, he found himself so depressed he could find very little reason to get out of bed in the morning. The extent of these emotions was not visible to anyone on the outside, and Fred worked hard to keep it that way. Certainly in Fred's case or cases like his, there has to be more than disrupted routines to explain this extreme level of culture shock. Fred and Jenny felt so frustrated, angry, and depressed that they seriously considered packing up and heading home. And Fred and Jenny are not alone. On average, about one in five Americans leaves the foreign assignment prematurely due to adjustment problems.

The powerful cause of these severe reactions stems from something that is generally quite sensitive for everyone-- ego. Maintaining and repairing one's ego, self-image, or identity is the most important underlying process in cross-cultural adjustment. For most of us there is nothing so fragile and important as our ego. Though it may not seem obvious, routines are a great source of maintaining our sense of self. A routine demonstrates of a level of proficiency, a proficiency that by the nature of its routinization is usually taken-for-granted. There is nothing like living in a foreign culture, however, to challenge basic proficiencies and raise them from a "taken-for-granted" to a "very conscience" level. In fact, often the more taken-for-granted the proficiency, the more severe the reaction to or shock at its loss.

Let's consider some specific examples from the Bailey's case. Getting around in the city in which one lives is often a skill very much taken-for-granted. For Jenny, driving around Boston, despite heavy traffic, was something she simply took for granted. Getting lost on the Tokyo subway system and not being able to even go from her home to a friend's house was a severe shock to her self-image as an independent and capable person. For someone who had been to countless important dinners with clients and had developed a rather impressive ability to deal smoothly with these situations, the mistake of sticking his chopsticks in his rice was a significant blow to Fred's confidence and ego. For both Jenny and Fred, and others like them, foreign assignments provide a steady stream of incidents from the simple to the complex that challenge our self-image. We are constantly confronted with situations that send messages such as "You don't understand this," "Don't you know you can't do that?" "Even six-year-olds in this country know that," "You're an idiot."

Although these situations are encountered from almost the time people step off the plane, it takes awhile before they build up enough momentum to overpower the defense mechanisms everyone has to protect their ego and their self-image. This is why the first phase of cross-cultural adjustment is often referred to as the *honeymoon phase*.

At first, there are a variety of novel and fascinating things about the country. But as time goes on, these novelties are no longer novel, and the number and magnitude of incidents that take shots at our egos build up. As more and more of these incidents accumulate, we get worn down and can no longer ignore them.

Although the specific symptoms vary with individuals, and even within individuals from week to week, emotions such as anger and frustration are common. In addition, feelings of anxiety and depression are also prevalent as the positive self-image we try to maintain gets battered and our confidence crumbles. Quite often, instinctive defense mechanisms try to protect our ego by directing our frustration toward others. "I'm not the problem; it's this stupid country and their backward ways." So as a way to take the focus off ourselves and defend our identity, we blame others. Blaming others is one of the most common symptoms of culture shock. Stop by any gathering center for expatriates of the same nationality, and you are likely to find conversations peppered with statements such as the following:

- I can't believe how stupid these people are. Their addresses make absolutely no sense.

- These people think they're so superior to the rest of us. They really bug me.

- The local managers just don't understand anything outside their country.

- The locals are just plain lazy. It's impossible to motivate them, and they feel no loyalty to the company.

- This whole thing is my spouse's fault. He has no appreciation for what I'm going through. He has his comfortable little cocoon at the office.

- My spouse has no appreciation for what I'm going through. Work is hell in this country. Just try to get something done. It takes forever.

Unfortunately, many people never recover from culture shock. Some return home, but not most. Most stay for the duration of their overseas assignment, even if they never fully recover from culture shock. Usually they stay because they are afraid of the negative consequences of returning early, or sometimes they simply hope things will get better with time. They end up, however, costing themselves and their companies. Given that they are just treading water until they can go home, they rarely do a great job. As a consequence, rarely do they return home to a great reward.

Most who stay eventually work their way through the culture shock stage and gradually adjust to living and working overseas. Although the pain of making mistakes is the primary source of culture shock, it can also be the source of adjustment as well. For example, it is unlikely that Fred will stick his chopsticks in his rice in future meetings with Japanese clients. Consequently, after this and numerous other mistakes are made, and most important, recognized, they are less likely to be repeated in the future or to become a source of frustration or embarrassment. Gradually, through making mistakes, recognizing them, and observing and learning appropriate behaviors, we learn what to do and not do and when to do or not do it.

In fact, this is one of the keys to effective cross-cultural adjustment. You need to take the attitude "I am going to make mistakes. I will probably even unintentionally embarrass myself and others. But that's great! I'll learn from each mistake and move on." This type of attitude not only raises the chances that you will recognize and admit mistakes you make, but it will help ensure that you indeed learn from them, that you don't get as frustrated, angry, defensive, or depressed as you might otherwise, and consequently, that you adjust more quickly and to a higher degree.

Summary

In summary, let's go over some key aspects about the cross-cultural adjustment. First, people establish routines in order to obtain a certain level of predictability in their life and to achieve a certain level of "psychological economy." These routines provide an important means of preserving and maintaining egos and identity. Living and working in new cultures generally disrupts these established routines. The more routines that are disrupted, the more severely any given routine is altered, and the more the disrupted routines are important ones, the greater the time and mental energy required to cope with the change, and the greater the culture shock and feelings of frustration, anger, and anxiety. Most important, however, is the fact that the disruption of routines challenges an individual's confidence, ego, and self-esteem. It is primarily threats to these sensitive aspects of all people that create the strongest emotional reactions associated with culture shock, such as depression, anger, denial, and even hatred. In principle, then, factors that increase the disruption of routines and uncertainty tend to inhibit cross-cultural adjustment, while factors that reduce disruption and uncertainty tend to facilitate cross-cultural adjustment.

With the basic process of culture shock and adjustment outlined, we can now turn our attention to specific strategies for adjusting more effectively.

FACTORS INFLUENCING EXPATRIATE CROSS-CULTURAL ADJUSTMENT

This process of adjusting to foreign cultures consists of two interrelated components. The first component involves creating a new set of mental road maps and a book of traffic rules. These mental maps and rules enable us to predict what behaviors are expected in specific situations, how people will likely respond, what behaviors are not appropriate, and so on. These mental maps and rules allow us to control our environment better by being able to predict what to do and how to behave in a variety of situations.

The second and related component involves mastering the new expected behaviors. For example, it is one thing to know Japanese communicate in a more indirect fashion, but it is quite another thing to be able to change your communication behavior from a direct to a more indirect style. The challenge is equally difficult for the Japanese in changing from their indirect style to a more direct one when transferred to countries such as Germany or Canada.

Simplified, cross-cultural adjustment involves figuring out what the new road maps and traffic rules are in the foreign culture, and then developing the driving skills necessary to get you safely where you want to go.

Although we tend to think about cross-cultural adjustment generically, we actually adjust to three separate aspects--work, social interaction, and the general environment. The reason for making this three-part distinction is that factors can affect one aspect of adjustment more than others.

Adjustment to the Job

The first dimension is the adjustment to the job to which you are assigned. Generally, this is the easiest of the three dimensions of adjustment. This is primarily because many of the procedures, policies, and requirements of the task are the same or very similar between the foreign operation and the home-country operation. However, although this is the easiest of the three dimensions, it is not necessarily an easy adjustment. Even if some of the policies and procedures are the same, the corporate culture of the foreign operation and the host-country culture can be dramatically different from that of the parent company and the home culture. These cultural differences can significantly affect how tasks get done.

Consequently, although you may be sent from Toronto to Hong Kong to perform basically the same task performed at home, elements of the foreign operation and the host-country culture may make it necessary to perform the task in a slightly, or even dramatically, different manner in order to achieve similar results and success. For example, a systems engineer in Canada may be able to simply interview workers in order to find out their needs and uses of a proposed computer program. However, in India, workers may only expect to be told how they are to use the new program and may be confused by interviews asking for their input. Consequently, you may find that simply asking Indian workers how they would use the program generates information that is incomplete and inaccurate.

Adjustment to Interacting with Host Nationals

The second dimension is adjusting to interaction with host nationals. If you're like most people, this will be the most difficult of the three adjustment dimensions. This is primarily because it is in interactions with host nationals that differences in mental road maps and traffic rules show up and cause accidents.

Remember Fred Bailey, our "innocent" in Japan? Fred had an experience that illustrates how different mental road maps and traffic rules make interpersonal cross-cultural adjustment difficult. Not long after his arrival in Japan, Fred had a meeting with representatives of a top-100 Japanese multinational firm concerning a potentially large contract. Fred, the lead American consultant for the potential contract, Ralph Webster, and one of the senior Japanese associate consultants, Kenichi Kurokawa, who spoke perfect English, met with a team from the Japanese firm. The Japanese team consisted of four members — the vice president of administration, the director of international personnel, and two staff specialists. After some awkward handshakes and bows, Fred said he knew the Japanese gentlemen were busy and he didn't want to waste their time, so he would get right to the point. Fred then had the other American lay out their firm's proposal for the project and what the project would cost. After the presentation, Fred asked the Japanese for their reaction to the proposal. The Japanese did not respond immediately, and so Fred launched into his summary version of the proposal, thinking that the translation might have been insufficient. But again, the Japanese had only the vaguest of responses to his direct questions.

Five months passed after the first meeting, and a contract between the firms was yet to be signed. "I can never seem to get a direct response from Japanese," Fred complained.

Fred decided that not much progress was being made with the client because he and his group just didn't know enough about the client to package the proposal in a way that was appealing. Consequently, he called in the senior American associated with the proposal, Ralph Webster, and asked him to develop a report on the client so the proposal could be reevaluated and changed where necessary. Jointly, they decided that one of the more promising young Japanese research associates, Tashiro Watanabe, would be the best person to take the lead on this report. To impress upon Tashiro the importance of this task and the great potential they saw in him, they decided to have the young Japanese associate meet with both Fred and Ralph. In the meeting, Fred had Ralph lay out the nature and importance of the task. At which point Fred leaned forward in his chair and said, "You can see that this is an important assignment and that we are placing a lot of confidence in you by giving it to you. We need the report by this time next week so that we can revise and re-present our proposal. Can you do it?" After a somewhat pregnant pause, Tashiro responded hesitantly, "I'm not sure what to say." At that point Fred smiled, got up from his chair and walked over to the young Japanese associate, extended his hand, and said, "Hey, there's nothing to say. We're just giving you the opportunity you deserve."

The day before the report was due, Fred asked Ralph how the report was coming. Ralph said that since he had heard nothing from Tashiro, he assumed everything was under control, but that he would double-check. Ralph later ran into one of the American research associates, John Maynard. Ralph knew that John had been hired because of his Japanese fluency, and that unlike any of the other Americans, John often went out after work with some of the Japanese research associates including Tashiro. So Ralph asked John if he knew how Tashiro was coming on the report. John then recounted that last night at the office Tashiro had asked if Americans sometimes fired employees for being late with reports. John had sensed that this was more than a hypothetical question and asked Tashiro why he wanted to know. Tashiro did not respond immediately, and since it was 8:30 in the evening, John suggested they go out for a drink. At first Tashiro resisted, but then John assured him that they would grab a drink at a nearby bar and come right back. At the bar, John got Tashiro to open up.

Tashiro explained the nature of the report that he had been requested to produce. Tashiro continued to explain that even though he had worked long into the night every night to complete the report, it was just impossible, and he had doubted from the beginning whether he could complete the report in a week. Furthermore, Mr. Kurokawa, who was four years senior to Tashiro, had originally been involved in the project, and apparently nothing had been said to him about Tashiro's assignment. This made Tashiro quite uncomfortable.

At this point Ralph asked John, "Why the hell didn't he say something in the first place?" Ralph didn't wait to hear whether John had an answer to his question or not. He headed straight to Tashiro's desk.

The incident just got worse from that point. Ralph chewed Tashiro out and then went to Fred to explain that the report would not be ready and that Tashiro hadn't thought it could be from the start. "Then why didn't he say something?" Fred asked. No one had any answers and the whole thing just left everyone more suspect and uncomfortable with each other.

Adjustment to the General Environment

The third dimension of cross-cultural adjustment is adjustment to the general, nonwork environment. This is the dimension that has typically been the focus of many cross-cultural adjustment researchers and books. This dimension includes such issues as food, transportation, entertainment, and health-care. In terms of difficulty, this dimension generally falls between job and interaction adjustment.

Consider the encounter the Baileys had with a Japanese hot spring resort. Everyone in the office had advised Fred to stay at a famous hot spring north of Tokyo. Fred and his family arrived and were preparing to proceed to the front desk to check in when an elderly Japanese man started making gestures with his hands and speaking rapidly in Japanese. Fred and Jenny had stopped in time, but the two girls had stepped up to the main floor with their shoes on before the man could bring them their slippers. Once everyone had their multicolored slippers on and their shoes securely stored in the lockers, the Bailey clan proceeded to check in at the front desk.

This accomplished, two elderly Japanese women escorted the Baileys to their room. After walking down a long hall, the women stopped in front of a wood door, slid it back, and waited for the Baileys to enter. The hall door opened up into a small entry room about three feet wide and five feet long. The Japanese women indicated that they should all remove their slippers, but the girls had opened the inner entry door and stepped up into the room.

After removing their slippers, Fred and Jenny gazed in amazement at their room, because that was all it was — one big, nearly empty room. The Japanese women showed the Baileys the closet in which the futons (sleeping mattresses and blankets) were stored, and rattled off several things in Japanese.

As the Japanese women prepared to leave, Fred tried to give them a tip. Both simply covered their mouths and waved their right hands back and forth in front of their faces.

Later Fred decided to be brave and soak in one of the hot springs. He went downstairs to the locker room and undressed. Strangely, there were two doors leading out of the locker room. Unfortunately, the signs above each door were in Japanese. Fred decided to take the door on the right. Fred entered a large room. On the right side was a line of short wooden stools and small buckets in front of a row of what looked like water facets. At one of the facets, a Japanese man was seated and was vigorously washing his hair. In the center of the room was a large "tub" about the size of a swimming pool. By the time Fred noticed this, he also noticed the giggles coming from three young women sitting in the water on the left of the tub. Fred had inadvertently wandered into the "coed" bathing area.

Later that evening, Fred and his family decided to have a fresh fish dinner. After a few strange appetizers, a big fish was brought in on a large platter. As the fish was placed on a table in front of the Baileys, Fred noticed a movement. As he looked closer, Fred could see the gills of the fish slowly opening and closing in a futile attempt to breath. The body of the fish had been masterfully sliced, and little filets lay along its torso. Christine shrieked, "Daddy its still alive! They've sliced it open, and its still alive!" Suddenly, everyone lost their appetite.

Summary of Influential Factors

As we mentioned, some factors have more influence on one aspect of cross-cultural adjustment than the others. We have already covered many of the factors in previous chapters. Consequently, the table on the following page simply provides a listing of the various factors and their relative influence on each of the three aspects of cross-cultural adjustment.

Factors Impacting Cross-Cultural Adjustment

FACTOR	IMPACT ON ADJUSTMENT		
	Work Adjustment	Interaction Adjustment	General Adjustment
Personal Characteristics (Discussed in chapter two)	Moderate	Major	Moderate
Cultural Distance (Degree of difference between "home" and "host" cultures)	Moderate	Major	Moderate
Training (Both pre- and postarrival)	Major	Major	Major
Previous Experience (In any other foreign country)	Minor	Minor	Moderate
Overlap with Predecessor	Major	Minor	Minor
Logistical Support ("Look-See" visit, etc.)	Minor	Minor	Moderate
Job Autonomy (Degree of freedom & discretion)	Major	Minor	Minor
Job Clarity (Clarity of tasks and roles)	Major	Minor	Minor
Social Support	Minor	Moderate	Minor

FACTORS INFLUENCING SPOUSE CROSS-CULTURAL ADJUSTMENT

Compared to employees, spouses have a bigger cross-cultural adjustment challenge. While employees have the built-in structure of an organization and job, spouses generally are left on their own to figure out how to survive and succeed in the new environment and culture. Even spouses who worked full-time before the assignment are often unable to do so during the assignment because of visa restrictions. This often leaves them feeling isolated and alone.

In our research and experience, we have found that although expatriate candidates are often excited about the career potential of an international assignment, spouses may not be. For spouses, a move to a foreign country may simply represent a disruption of their own career or long-term social relationships. Not surprisingly, then, we found that the more a spouse is in favor of accepting the assignment, the more the spouse tries to learn about the country and culture of the assignment. In turn, this self-initiated predeparture preparation is positively related to interaction adjustment. Interestingly, spouses who have high levels of adjustment are also those who have been interviewed by the firm prior to the overseas assignment.

Given the ego-bashing, or at least bruising, effect of cross-cultural adjustment, both family and host country national social support helps spouse interaction adjustment. Host national support particularly helps spouse interaction adjustment. This is primarily because host country nationals provide both a source of emotional support and an effective source of information about the culture. In addition, they can provide feedback on how the spouse is doing and what changes can be made to function more effectively in the culture.

As in the case of the employee, the greater the differences between the home and host cultures, the greater the difficulty of spouse adjustment to the general environment. The more the home culture of the spouse and the host culture of the assignment differ, the more difficult it is to figure out the cultural road maps and traffic rules, and the more difficult it is to operate effectively, even after figuring them out.

Even though some spouses who worked full-time before the international assignment find work during the assignment, overall, most spouses do not work during the international assignment. As we mentioned, this is often due to government restrictions in the host country. Consequently, most spouses have to deal with the general living conditions all day, every day. It is perhaps not surprising that living conditions in the overseas post that are equal to or better than those prior to the assignment help spouse general-environment adjustment, while worse living conditions negatively affect general adjustment.

STEPS TO TAKE FOR SUCCESSFUL CROSS-CULTURAL ADJUSTMENT

For you, a key question is what steps can I take to maximize my chances of success and minimize my chance of failure? This question is especially important given that some of the factors that affect cross-cultural adjustment that we have discussed are not within your control. For example, the level of organization or country culture novelty (or uniqueness) are not really within anyone's control. So what effective steps can be taken?

Selection and Training

Although we have already talked about selection and training, two things are worth emphasizing. First, if you are like 85% of candidates for international assignments, you are married. The evidence suggests that the opinion of your spouse can significantly affect both self-initiated predeparture training and in-country adjustment. Yet only about 30 percent of European and U.S. firms take the opportunity to discuss spouses' opinions concerning the possible international assignment. It may be beneficial to provide your spouse with an opportunity to talk with someone in your firm about the company's international assignment practices and policies. Second, although you cannot control the extent of organization or country culture novelty (or uniqueness), you can factor it into your acceptance decision and training requests. The greater the culture novelty, the more carefully you should look at your personal characteristics relative to cross-cultural adjustment, and the more predeparture and postarrival training you should request.

Job Design

Our research and experience also makes it clear that greater job discretion and clarity, and less role conflict facilitate work adjustment. But what can you do to ensure adequate job discretion, make role expectations clear, and eliminate conflicting demands?

Let's consider the issue of role clarity. One of the easiest, but rarely used, techniques for increasing role clarity is job overlap. If at all possible, request (insist upon?) several days or perhaps weeks of overlap time with your predecessor. During this time, you can learn some of "the ropes." The more complex the job and the less experienced you are at the specific job, the longer and more necessary the overlap. In interviews, expatriates specifically mention that overlap is a relative low-cost means of facilitating expatriate adjustment and effectiveness. In countries such as Japan, Korea, Saudi Arabia, France, and many Latin American countries, this overlap is necessary for you to get properly introduced to customers, suppliers, and government officials.

Let's assume the incumbent is capable of clarifying the new job. This does not necessarily lead to a reduction in role conflict. It is quite possible, and not uncommon, for clarification of the job expectations to lead to a clarification of previously hidden role conflicts. The primary source of role conflict for expatriates is conflicting expectations between the parent firm and the local operation. Consequently, clarifying the job may serve to uncover conflicting expectations from the parent and local foreign organizations. Thus, first gain a solid understanding of the expectations of the parent firm and the local operation, and where conflicts exist Next, determine the underlying objectives of both organizations. Finally, see if there is a way to satisfy both.

However, despite your best efforts to clarify your role and reduce conflicts, you may not be able to eliminate conflicts. This is probably why role discretion is the single strongest factor on work adjustment. Even if role ambiguity and conflict exist, having a fair amount of freedom to decide what tasks to do, how to do them, when to do them, and who should do them facilitates your ability to cope effectively with ambiguity and conflict. Thus the way to solve all of these problems is easy. Simply try to get as much role discretion and freedom as possible.

To facilitate your efforts in clarifying your role, reducing conflict, and increasing your autonomy and freedom, consider the following questions:

1. Why are you being sent to this particular post? (Because there are no host nationals capable of fulfilling the job? To provide you with a needed developmental experience?)

2. What are the criteria by which success in the job will be measured? What is really desired of you?

3. Are the objectives and goals between the parent firm and the local unit consistent? Between the local unit and the particular department in which you will be working?

4. How much coordination and control are needed between the parent firm and the local operation? Is the amount of discretion in the particular position in question consistent with the coordination needs?

Social Support

Social support can facilitate cross-cultural adjustment for both you and your spouse. Social support from host country nationals has a particularly strong impact on interaction adjustment. Although you cannot directly control the amount of social support you receive, you can take steps to enhance the probability of receiving it. Some firms have adopted the practice of asking a host country national employee and family within the local foreign operation to help the expatriate and family have a "soft landing." Generally, this assistance has focused on logistical issues such as housing, schools, and shopping. Although friendships cannot be mandated by the firm, some companies have made it clear that helping families (especially spouses) become involved in social or cultural activities is appreciated. You might ask your firm about this type of idea and ask for a "sponsoring" host national employee. Other firms have taken a more indirect approach and simply provide stacks of information on local social and cultural activities and groups with which expatriate managers and families might become involved. If your firm seems reluctant to "assign" a host or sponsoring family, make sure you ask for general information that will help you meet local nationals both inside and especially outside your company.

CONCLUSION

This chapter and chapter five outline a definition of culture, a process of adjustment, and a set of specific factors that provide a beginning framework for understanding the complexities of successfully moving human resources around the world. We have pointed to the difficulty and importance of understanding and adjusting to the invisible aspects of culture and the factors that can either enhance or detract from that process, and have argued that factors such as organization and country culture novelty, which are not in your direct control, should at least be factored into decisions that are within your control. You may be tired of hearing it, but it's hard to overemphasize the point that you need to be proactive in getting the support and help you need to be successful. Do not count on or wait for your company to take the initiative. Hopefully, you now have an even greater number of issues on which to focus your proactivity.

Chapter Eight

How Do I Make the Return a Success?

Hopefully, you're reading this chapter before you ever land in the country of your international assignment. If so, you'll want to read this chapter now and refer back to it at least once or twice each year during your assignment. Toward the end of your assignment, go through this chapter once again carefully and also complete the self- and career-assessment exercises in the companion workbook. If you are about to return or have recently returned from an international assignment, hopefully you took our advice at the beginning of the book and started by reading this chapter first.

THE DIFFICULTY OF
REPATRIATION ADJUSTMENT

In any case, the return from an international assignment is perhaps the most critical point in the process. Like the space shuttle returning from an important mission, successful reentry is critical to your overall success. If the reentry doesn't go well, much of the benefit of the mission is lost. What most people don't realize about the space shuttle is that the window of successful reentry is actually quite narrow—too steep a reentry and the shuttle would burn up, too shallow and it would skip off the earth's atmosphere and bounce back into space. To place it in perspective, imagine the earth is about the size of a basketball. Now imagine placing the edge of a single sheet of paper against the basketball. In relative terms, the thickness of a single sheet of paper next to a basketball is about how narrow the feasible reentry window is for the space shuttle when it returns to earth.

In presenting this analogy, we *do not* want to create images of gloom and doom, or say that successful repatriation is impossible—quite the contrary. Instead, we simply want to impress upon you the importance of repatriation and how challenging it can be.

Many people think, "Repatriation—challenging? I'm coming home. What's the big deal?" It turns out that repatriation adjustment is not only more challenging and difficult than expected, but for most people, repatriation adjustment is actually more difficult than adjustment to the original overseas assignment. In fact, in one study we did of American, Japanese, and Finnish managers returning to their home country after an international assignment, we found that most managers had more difficulty adjusting to being back home than they did to being overseas.

Repatriation Culture Shock

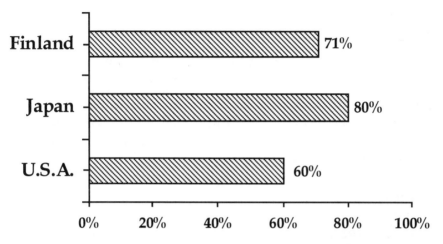

Note: This chart shows the percentage of managers who found repatriation adjustment more difficult than the original adjustment overseas.

So while we don't want to create images of gloom and doom, we also don't want to underplay the challenges of successful repatriation. The following quotes come from managers just like yourself and are worth considering.

> Be mentally prepared for enormous change when coming home. Expect repatriation culture shock to surpass the culture shock you might have experienced when you went overseas.
>
> –American expatriate returning from a
> seven-year assignment in Indonesia

> Coming back home was more difficult than going abroad because you expect changes when going overseas. It was real culture shock during repatriation. *I was an alien in my home country.* My own attitudes had changed so that it was

difficult to understand my own old customs. Old friends had moved, had children, or just vanished. Others were interested in our experiences, but only sort of. They simply couldn't understand our experiences overseas, or they just envied our way of life.

–Expatriate spouse returning from a three-year assignment in Vietnam

In talking with repatriating managers, we have been asked a variety of questions. However, most of them fall into two categories. We have come to call them the "So What?" and "So Why?" questions. People asking the "So What?" question typically ask something like *"So what* if repatriation adjustment is a little more difficult? Why is that important?" People asking the "So Why?" question typically ask something like, *"So why* is repatriation so difficult?" In this chapter, we try to answer both questions. Let's begin by addressing the "So what?" question, and then we'll address the "So why?" question.

IMPORTANCE OF REPATRIATION ADJUSTMENT

Repatriation adjustment is important for two basic reasons. First, it has a big impact on your work performance back home, and second, it has an impact on your overall happiness.

Repatriation Adjustment and Work Performance

Let's first look at the relationship between repatriation adjustment and work performance. When we talked with managers before their return home, many have made statements similar to the following: "So what if my family and I have difficulty readjusting? We'll get over it, right?" Probably, but the cost of poor or slow readjustment can be high in terms of work performance. This happens for several reasons.

First, we need to keep in mind that your work performance evaluation is a function of two distinct but related factors: absolute level of performance, and time-related expectations of performance.

Clearly, your performance evaluation will be a function of your absolute level of performance on the job. If you are doing a poor job at accomplishing required tasks or are not meeting objectives, this will have a negative impact on your performance evaluation. Obviously, the reverse will also be true.

However, of equal importance in your evaluation is where performance is expected to be at a given point in time. Suppose, for example, that you expect employees to take six months to master a specific task. Would you label them as "unsatisfactory" if they had not mastered it in two months? What if you expected them to master the task in one month and they had not achieved that level of performance after two months? Would you then label them unsatisfactory? So you can see, the evaluation of anyone's performance is partly a function of what level of performance you expect at a given point in time.

Putting these two aspects together, your job performance after repatriation will be a function of how well you do the job in absolute terms, and how quickly you master the job in relative terms. It is the second part of this that is most problematic during repatriation. Why? Because virtually everyone will expect you to readjust quickly and automatically, especially those who have *not* lived overseas before (which in many companies is the vast majority of people). Consequently, little "down time" is given, and returning employees are often expected to hit the ground running. The following quotes from recently repatriated managers illustrate this expectation:

> Arrived home on Saturday. Started work at 150% on Monday. I have worked constant seventy-hour weeks since.

> I arrived home on Tuesday and started work on Wednesday and have been working ten to twelve-hour hour days since. I haven't adjusted yet to much of anything and really feel depressed.

> I worked fourteen-hour days, six days a week. There was little time to look for housing, yet the company still pressured me to move out of a hotel in order to get me off the 'expense' status.

Given that many people will expect you to hit the ground running, repatriation adjustment difficulties can significantly and negatively affect both formal, and perhaps more important, informal performance evaluations. This is critical, because as we pointed out most managers have more difficulty coming home than going overseas.

If you are married and have a family, it's not just your own repatriation adjustment that could affect your work performance; your family's reentry adjustment could affect it as well. Based on our research and experience, your family's *successful* repatriation adjustment will have a neutral to positive "spillover" effect on your job performance; repatriation adjustment *difficulties* will have a moderate to strong negative effect on your job performance. The realities of adjustment spillover and work performance are emphasized in this expatriate's experience:

My spouse has had a very difficult time coming home from Europe and living in the suburbs of America. She hates it. Her adjustment difficulty has made my life less than wonderful and my work performance less than excellent.

So the first answer to the "So what?" question about the difficulty of repatriation adjustment is clear. Personal or family repatriation adjustment difficulties matter because they can significantly affect your job performance and evaluations.

Repatriation Adjustment and Happiness

The second answer to the "So what?" question is found in the relationship between personal and family repatriation adjustment and your general level of satisfaction and happiness. Although many of us try to keep work and personal and family life separate, the reality is that complete separation is almost never possible. In the case of repatriating managers, our research and experience clearly show that the spillover effects are huge.

First, repatriation difficulties and job performance problems at work have a significant and negative effect on personal and family happiness. For example, the fact that your boss may have no appreciation for the challenges of returning home after an international assignment can easily enhance frustrations and irritability, and try your and your family's patience. Just think about it; how happy have you been in your personal or family life in the past when things were going badly at work?

Obviously, if difficulties at work during repatriation can affect your happiness, then readjustment difficulties in your family can also affect your overall happiness. When was the last time your spouse was really miserable and you were really happy?

The point of all this is that not only is repatriation more difficult than most people expect, but these difficulties have significant effects on your work performance and personal happiness. It's important to understand thoroughly the factors that affect repatriation adjustment. This is what we want to do in the next section.

DIMENSIONS OF REPATRIATION ADJUSTMENT

Before we get directly into the factors that affect repatriation adjustment, let us discuss briefly the dimensions of repatriation adjustment. Although we talk about it as though it were one generic "thing," there are actually three related but distinct dimensions of repatriation adjustment. First, you will need to adjust to a new job and work environment. This aspect of repatriation adjustment is not as easy as you might think. Even though the average expatriate has almost fifteen years of experience in his or her company, he or she still makes comments like "Be prepared for *corporate* culture shock when you come home!" One expatriate with twelve years experience in the parent company commented:

> Our organizational culture was turned upside-down. We now have a different strategic focus; different "tools" to get the job done; and different buzz words to make it happen. I had to learn a whole new corporate "language."

Work-related adjustment challenges during repatriation are one of the most frequently mentioned problems by repatriating managers.

Second, you and your family need to adjust to communicating with home country coworkers and friends. After a three- to five-year year international assignment, home country nationals often seem like foreigners to you, and you will certainly seem strange to them. Living with yourself every day during the several years on assignment, you will unlikely notice changes in your perspectives, behaviors, or even values. Others, however, remember you before the assignment, and then see you after a two-, three-, four-year or longer gap. The contrast for them can be dramatic.

Finally, you and your family face the problem of readjusting to the general living environment (food, weather, housing, transportation, schools, and so on). These adjustments to the "general" culture are often the most challenging, as reflected by the fact that two-thirds of the European and U.S. expatriates experience significant general environment repatriation adjustment problems. The following comment describes some of the specific dilemmas of coming home:

> It was challenging to return home and find housing, locate shopping stores, and make friends. Even though I'd lived in the same metro area and country before, this was like moving into a new world, and I had to start from scratch. I never realized that returning "home" would not be instantly "home."

FACTORS INFLUENCING REPATRIATION ADJUSTMENT

Now that we have established that repatriation involves adjusting to three related but separate dimensions, we can focus on factors that influence adjustment to any one dimension or even all three dimensions. To place these factors in context, we need to keep in mind that repatriation adjustment actually begins before you ever get on the plane to go home. You will begin to make changes in your mental maps of what work and living will be back home *before* you actually return. Such changes in mental maps are generally helpful if you have an accurate idea of what to expect. Accordingly, several potential sources of accurate information about the home country can help modify and mold your mental maps of the home country terrain *before* you actually return.

Sponsors

A formally or informally assigned sponsor can provide you with important information about structural changes, strategic shifts, political coups at work, promotion opportunities, and general job- and company-related knowledge. This information helps with adjustment to the job and organization more than adjustment to the general environment. Without an effective sponsor during and after international assignments, you can be caught in the following repatriate's dilemma after spending nine years in Venezuela:

> Fitting in is difficult if you have been gone a long time and have no ongoing contacts. There is tremendous insecurity, since no one knows you or cares, and you can easily get caught in the next job reduction plan. Some reward for all the sacrifice of going abroad!

In this repatriate's case, an effective sponsor might have reduced some of the apparent problems the expatriate encountered during reentry. Even though sponsors can provide important adjustment-related information during international assignments and helpful support during repatriation, relatively few expatriates actually have such sponsors throughout an assignment. In fact, only 22% of American expatriates have sponsors while on foreign assignment.

Home Leave

Another important source of information about the home country and company is periodic visits to the home country during an international assignment.   These visits provide you and your family the opportunity to acquire information about changes at work, friends, and the home country throughout the course of an international assignment. Conversely, these visits also allow co-workers and friends to observe the changes in you throughout the assignment. While 65% of the U.S. expatriates receive paid home leave for themselves and their families throughout the international assignment, a study by ORC (Organization Resources Councilors) of approximately 250 American and Canadian multinational firms found that only 35% of expatriates and families are required to take their home leave at home.   As a result, the net informational and networking benefits of home leaves are often left overseas as expatriates use home leave money for trips to more exotic places than home.

Repatriation Training

Prereturn training and orientation programs provided by the firm are another source of information before returning home.   Repatriates we have surveyed and interviewed comment consistently on the importance of such training. In fact, except for locating an appropriate job after an international assignment, taking advantage of training during repatriation is the most frequent suggestion made by repatriating managers.   This training can potentially facilitate adjustment not only at work, but in communicating with home-country nationals and living in the new environment.

Given the positive impact on adjustment that prereturn training can have, it is unfortunate that relatively few multinational firms provide training or orientation during repatriation. In fact, 64% of American expatriates receive *absolutely no training* before returning to their home country. Furthermore, approximately 90% of all spouses receive no repatriation training—and these percentages are not much better for European or Asian firms. After returning home, one spouse suggested that "a repatriation meeting should be provided to families like the orientation meeting before going overseas since many changes occur at home in a three- to five-year period." Without such training, many expatriates and spouses inefficiently search for, and often don't find, accurate information about their home country during repatriation.

To be effective, however, the training does not need to occur before your return. In fact, our research and experience increasingly suggests that attending even a one-day program within the first six weeks after you return home can be very valuable. If you have the opportunity, look for a program that focuses on the general dynamics of repatriation adjustment and includes instructors who have personally been through the process. If you have a family, take advantage of any training offered to them, especially if you have children older than twelve. Teenagers often have significant difficulties in repatriation adjustment. While you and I might not experience significant social consequences from not knowing the latest slang or music groups, teenagers can pay a heavy price. Lack of understanding the dynamics of repatriation will only add to their frustrations and anxiety.

Return Job

For you, one of the most pivotal components of a successful repatriation experience is the selection of your return job assignment. However, only 4.3% of the North American multinational firms studied by ORC gave more than six-months' notice to expatriates that they would be returning home;   30% received approximately three-months' notice; 64% received random notification reflecting little planning for repatriation. This relatively short-term return horizon is also reflected in the significantly negative job experiences of some repatriates we studied.

> After being home three months I am still waiting for a permanent office. All this after thirty years of experience in the company and three international assignments!
> –Expatriate with extensive experience

> No one accepted responsibility for placing me back in the organization.   I ended up without a job when I was expecting a promotion! My wife also gave up her job with the same company to go overseas (she had twelve years of experience).   We were promised a job for her upon our return. Again, no one has helped us find one.
> –Expatriate with fifteen years of experience in the parent company

> The major problem of repatriation was in the area of locating my next position after returning home. It was totally up to me and networking connections. The official process STINKS!
> –Expatriate with sixteen years of experience in the parent company

From these accounts, it is clear that the first step in effective adjustment at work is having meaningful work! However, approximately two out of three expatriates from Europe, Asia, or the U.S. don't even know what their return assignment will be before they return. Because return assignments are not planned, expatriates often talk about being in a "holding pattern" with no place to land.

While human resources and other executives have good intentions to help you, and want your repatriation to be a success, ultimately you should consider it your responsibility and opportunity. You need to make sure that you are proactive in finding a place to land.

Repatriation Job Uncertainty

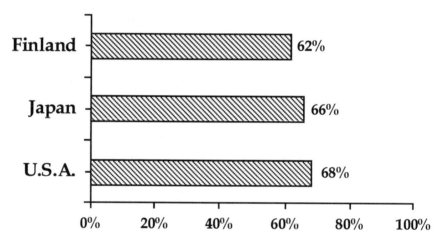

Note: This chart shows the percentage of repatriates who did not know what their job would be just before returning home.

It should come as no surprise that when expatriates do get a job after returning home, these positions are sometimes not optimal. In fact, sometimes they are ill-defined, low impact, "make-work" positions intended to keep expatriates occupied until a more suitable job can be found. The problem is that no one wants to take you on if you are now in a "nothing" job. Those who don't know you may wonder, "If you were really good, would you be in a 'nothing' job?"

More unfortunately still, when permanent positions are located, they are often positions with reduced autonomy and authority in comparison to positions expatriates held during their most recent overseas assignment.

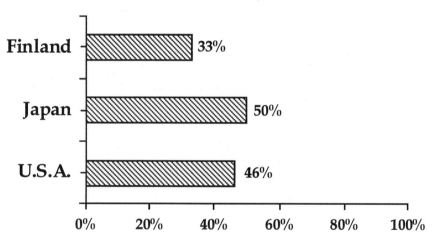

Reduced Autonomy at Work

Note: This chart shows the percentage of managers who experience less autonomy in their return jobs compared to their overseas position.

Specifically, 46% of American managers have less autonomy and authority back home, as these comments by a recently returned banker illustrate.

> When I was overseas, I felt I had an impact on the business. In the U.S., I feel as though the impact . . . if any . . . is minimal . . . When I came home, I was assigned to a newly

created, undefined staff job where I had no friends, no contacts, and no access to management. Firms need to realize that expatriates have developed independent decision-making skills, become accustomed to having final authority, and conditioned to having their business judgment given a lot of credibility by top management. In my new job, my business judgment is much less valued than when I was overseas. Until firms change, expatriates should expect the worst when coming home, to avoid disappointment.

–American expatriate with a large commercial bank

Many expatriates take an international assignment with hopes that it will result in a promotion after successfully working overseas. Unfortunately, this is not how it always works out:

I went on my foreign assignment to the UK as a favor for the department. In return I received nothing special for the ten months I spent away from my family and the hardship I put them through. I really expected a promotion after coming back home and did not receive it.

In reality, most expatriates returning home do not receive a promotion over the position they held during the international assignment; a majority actually move into lower positions. To some extent this may be unavoidable. However, managers we have interviewed and surveyed comment that the opportunity to use the knowledge and skills they gained overseas is more important than the actual level of the position.

By the end of your international assignment, you will have gained unique country knowledge, language proficiency, and international management skills. In fact, one of the strategic purposes of international assignments is to develop these skill and knowledge areas. Unfortunately, without careful planning and conscious effort, these skills may not be put to use. Specifically, in one study we conducted, only one-third of European and American managers had the opportunity to use their international experience after repatriation. Without adequate planning, you may find yourself expressing sentiments similar to the following by two different expatriates:

> Firms must value international expertise . . . not only appreciate it, but actually put it to good use. Don't let a corporate headquarters' environment destroy the lessons, "business savvy," negotiation skills, and foreign language proficiencies which expatriates learned from the real world . . . a global marketplace.

> This company places little value on my international skills. In fact, I am now fluent in Japanese, but the company has shown no interest in placing me in a position to use my recently acquired language skills. What a waste!

Repatriation Process

The parent company's overall human resource approach to the repatriation process can have a significant impact on adjustment after expatriates return home. Sometimes the repatriation process is not as clearly defined and explained as it might be. Approximately 60% of American repatriates feel that the company communicated an unclear picture of the repatriation process. This overall sense of uncertainty is reflected in one American expatriate's experience: "What was it like coming home? No clear direction in my job, no clear direction in my career, and no assistance during the return. You are on your own around here!" Undoubtedly, your experience will be more positive than this, but you are the key person to ensure that it is.

Financial Considerations

In addition to clarifying the repatriation process, you need to pay special attention to financial readjustment. A majority of repatriates experience a decline in living standard after international assignments. Some of these financial dynamics are captured below.

> The cost of everything—from housing to the basic necessities—was so much higher in New York that it was, literally, shocking—even though we expected it. Everything is so expensive in New York City. In Mexico, and before that Brazil, my family and I lived quite well. After returning to the States, it was back to reality—purchases had to be budgeted, something we hadn't done for years.

> When you are overseas you receive many benefits, such as maybe a free car, or free petrol, or a nicer home than you have had back in your home country. You become accustomed to these benefits; then, when you return to your home country, things return "to normal," and lots of these benefits you were accustomed to disappear. It's like being Cinderella and midnight has struck!

It may seem like a silly thing, but many expatriates report that going back on a "budget" takes some adjustment, especially when they don't expect it to be an issue. For couples, this means they often don't talk about spending patterns until one or the other notices that they are running out of money before running out of month. This typically then leads to "expenditure disagreements" (read "fights about money"—how much is being spent, who's spending it, and on what). Often the other repatriation difficulties fan the flames of these "financial discussions" until they become quite heated.

Social Status

After coming home, expatriates and their families lose the formal status of being a "foreigner." Nearly 55% of the American expatriates and spouses experience a significant drop in social status. As one spouse said, "The biggest surprise of coming home was that I simply didn't realize how special we were being treated in all aspects of life during our international assignment."

During an overseas assignment, expatriates typically feel like a "big fish in a little subsidiary pond." After coming home, the role reverses to being a "little fish in a big corporate pond." As one expatriate returning from a nine-year executive position in the UK said, "If you have been the orchestra conductor overseas, it is very difficult to accept a position as second fiddle when coming home." In general, the drop in social status has a negative impact on adjustment at work and adjustment to the general environment.

Housing Conditions

In addition to social status shifts, changes in housing conditions can significantly influence repatriation adjustment for both you and your family. Satisfaction with housing conditions is related positively to all three facets of repatriation adjustment for the employee and general adjustment for the spouse. The three biggest determinants of dissatisfaction with housing are as follows: (1) repair costs for the home they rented out during the assignment (often exceeding $10,000), (2) having to move out of a hotel or other temporary housing before adequate permanent housing is found, and (3) finding oneself priced out of the market because of inflation for those that sold their home when they were sent overseas.

UNIQUE ASPECTS OF SPOUSE REPATRIATION ADJUSTMENT

Many of the predeparture and postarrival factors discussed are also relevant to spouses during repatriation. However, some important and unique aspects of a spouse's repatriation are a function of spouses' careers before, during, and after international assignments. Approximately 55% of American spouses work before, 12% during, and 30% after an international assignment.

> While my contacts and visits with work colleagues in the home country have been very occasional during the international assignment, the reestablishment of those contacts and returning to professional life has demanded even more effort than was required during expatriation.
>
> –Spouse returning from a four-year assignment in France

In many situations, spouses have difficulty finding work immediately after international assignments. Sometimes these challenges are related to the loss of professional skills or contacts. Others are challenged in the job-finding process when potential employers "wonder" if the spouse will go on another international assignment in the near future. Still others struggle with establishing the home and helping children adjust, which results in little time left over for the job-search. Given the potential difficulties in finding appropriate work after repatriation, it is important to take advantage of any job-finding assistance to spouses your firm might offer.

STEPS TOWARD SUCCESSFUL REPATRIATION ADJUSTMENT

Given the serious and costly problems associated with poor repatriation that might potentially leave you and your family "dangling in the wind," what can you do to create a strategic approach to the process of coming home and capture the full return on this important opportunity and investment?

Begin with the End in Mind

The best way to ensure that repatriation goes well is to begin with the end in mind. If you have an idea of what you hope to gain from the international experience and how you hope to leverage it afterwards, you will be well ahead of the crowd in facilitating your successful reentry.

The companion workbook provides some exercises to help you think more systematically about the globalization of your firm over the next several years, and your own development as a global leader. Completing this exercise in advance of even beginning your international assignment will help you think about where and how you can use the experience and knowledge you hope to gain after you return.

Keep Your Expectations Realistic

If you look at repatriation as a "homecoming," you're setting yourself up for failure. My company left me dangling in the wind, so to speak. I think that is wrong. I took a real demotion when we came home. No one in the company volunteered anything. I had to initiate everything. I fell through the cracks in the system . . . if indeed there was a repatriation system in this company. Why can't companies deal more efficiently and compassionately with employees returning from overseas assignments?

Many expatriates and their families expect a "hero's welcome" after returning home from a successful international assignment. This may be a bit unrealistic. Think about it for a minute. Did you roll out the red carpet for the last person you knew who returned from an international assignment? Most people will have no idea what you've been up to or how challenging it might have been. Some expatriates we have interviewed suggest that it might be more realistic to not really expect *any* welcome at all.

In fact, one American expatriate told us he actually lost his "identity" during repatriation. Apparently he did not exist on company records for up to three months after his return. He found out about the problem through a credit firm when he was denied two critical loans (house and car) because he was unemployed! This happened because the company had two separate human resource systems—one for international assignees and one for domestic employees—and he had not yet been put back on the domestic system when he applied for the loans. While this might be an atypical case, take care and consider the words of advice and warning from the following expatriate returning from a one-year assignment in England:

> Treat coming home as a "foreign assignment" and spend time getting the "lay of the land." Don't expect any special treatment—you're basically a "new hire." Look out for yourself.

Since you, the parent company, and home country have probably changed during the course of an international assignment, it is highly likely that numerous aspects of your perceptions of home are inaccurate. Accordingly, it is critical to manage and mold your own expectations and others' before you arrive home. By so doing, you will more likely have your expectations fulfilled, and you will more likely adjust effectively to work and nonwork issues after coming home.

Define the Strategic Function of Repatriation

The first step toward effective repatriation is an analysis of the strategic functions you can accomplish after you return home. Before the assignment, you should have defined the extent to which the assignment is designed to facilitate your development. If the strategic purpose of the international assignment was your development, the return assignment should be a critical next step in the development of additional executive skills and knowledge.

The companion workbook also has an exercise that you should complete just prior to your return. This exercise is designed to help you think about the next several steps in your career—where you want to go and what contributions you think you could make. Without a clear idea of the strategic role of your assignment and repatriation, you will likely be overwhelmed and will focus on all the immediate logistical aspects of the return.

Establish a Repatriation Team

After defining a clear strategic purpose for the return, put together your repatriation "team," consisting of a human resource department representative and either your supervisor (if located in the home country) or sponsor. You should work with these individuals to initiate preparations for your return at least six months before actual repatriation. If possible, look for a human resource department representative that has firsthand experience with the expatriation/repatriation process. Many expatriates have expressed this recommendation.

> It would have helped to *at least* have personnel people with *some* understanding of the experience of repatriation. Most of these people have *no* appreciation of what needs to be done when coming home. Since we had lived internationally and moved back one time before, we knew what to expect and basically had to manage it ourselves.

Either the supervisor or sponsor plays an important on this repatriation team in that they can be a great help in locating an appropriate return position for you. For example, the medical systems division of General Electric requires that sponsors play this active role in the repatriation process, and the sponsors are evaluated formally on the extent to which they effectively perform this function.

Sponsor Programs at GE Medical

GE has a well-developed system of sponsors. In some GE divisions this even involves a commitment to hire the expatriate manager back to a specific position before they even leave. More often, the system of assigned sponsor involves (1) assessing the expatriate's career objectives, (2) choosing a senior manager (often in the function to which the expatriate is likely to return) who is willing to serve as sponsor, (3) maintaining contact between the sponsor and expatriate throughout the assignment, including face-to-face meetings, (4) clarifying career objectives and capabilities before repatriation, (5) evaluating theperformance of the expatriate during the assignment, and (6) providing career advice as well as helping to find a position before the expatriate's repatriation.

Executives at several firms with sponsorship programs had additional advice. Overall, they recommended that the sponsor assignment should be systematic. First, the sponsor should be senior enough to the expatriate that the sponsor can provide a broad view of the organization. Second, the sponsor should be given specific guidelines about keeping in touch with the expatriate, such as form, content, and frequency of contacts. Too often, the sponsor is simply assigned, and that is it. If the sponsor takes the initiative and fulfills the responsibility, things go well. Otherwise the assigned sponsor is that in name only. Finally, the responsibility of planning for the expatriate manager's return and of finding a suitable position should not solely be that of the sponsor, but must be incorporated into the career systems of the firm.

Look at Your Situation

Once you have defined the strategic purposes for a return assignment and have your repatriation team in place, look at your situation and determine whether you fall in the "higher risk" category or not. Two main factors tend to place you at higher risk for repatriation difficulties. First, if you have extended international experience (either multiple assignments or a current assignment longer than five years), you will likely have more difficulty repatriating.

Generally, the longer you have been away from home, the more home is not home anymore, the more you are not the you you used to be, and the weaker your network of connections back into the organization. Second, if you are returning from an international assignment in a country very different from your home country (e.g., from Korea to the U.S.), you will likely encounter more difficulty than those returning from a more similar country (e.g., Canada). This is principally because the greater the cultural differences of the international assignment, the greater the changes that you have likely made in your behavior, perspectives, values, and attitudes. The more you have changed, the greater the likelihood that you will have some difficulty fitting back into the organization and the general environment.

Make Early Job Preparations

In order to avoid many of the problems associated with repatriation, consult your repatriation team to explore career path options after repatriation. To the extent possible, search out a return job that has a reasonable level of autonomy. While you would normally want that in a job, it's especially important after an international assignment. This is because during your international assignment you probably experienced considerable autonomy and came to enjoy that autonomy. In fact, many expatriates come to take the autonomy for granted. They forget what it's like to be encumbered with triple signatures and endless committee reviews. Finding a job with autonomy will certainly go a long way in facilitating your repatriation.

In addition to looking for a challenging job with discretion to make things happen, it is important to assess the skill match between what you have learned from the international assignment and how those skills could be used after returning home.   An exercise in the companion workbook provides a guide for assessing your new skills and knowledge, as well as reflecting on your new interests and future areas of development.   Obviously, if you can match your new skills and knowledge to a return job, you are much more likely to adjust to and do well in that job. As an excellent example, consider the following executive's experience after returning to Ford:

> After coming home, I took a position that gave me the opportunity to use what I learned while working at Mazda (majority-owned by Ford) in Japan for the last three years. The new job is terrific. Overall, coming home has been easy, since I returned to an area which deals specifically with international activities.   In my new group, it is critical to know how Mazda works, and I have that knowledge.

More important to the firm, though, the return assignment can accomplish a critical strategic objective: information transfer. In the above case, knowledge gained by the Ford expatriate was effectively used after the international assignment, and the people working with this individual gradually learned from him how to better deal with Mazda even though they had never worked in Japan.

For some firms and industries, it may not be possible for you to find the ideal job when you come home because of downsizing, restructuring, and so on. In this case, it is better to get a clear idea of this early rather than late. You may have to be aggressive in getting a realistic idea of the situation back home.   One expatriate with a large U.S. energy firm described this "mushroom-growing" approach to return assignments:

> Why can't firms provide at least some information about the progress, *or lack of it*, in finding a new assignment while expatriates are waiting to come home.

Correspondence I sent home from Jakarta during the last three months of our stay was never answered. Being in the dark for months is very hard when you know you are going to repatriate!

Basically, if there are not good jobs waiting for you when you return, you want to find out before you return. Otherwise, you will likely come home with inflated expectations that result in significant adjustment problems.

After you locate an appropriate job, take some time to consider the background and experience of your future supervisor and coworkers. Often, these people have little or no international experience, and consequently have difficulty understanding and working around the challenges of repatriation. On average, less than one-third of Americans repatriates have supervisors with international experience (about half the rate of Japanese and European repatriates). In some cases, domestically oriented supervisors and coworkers actually inhibited the adjustment process. For example, an American expatriate confided: "When I came home, coworkers were very jealous of my assignment even though my responsibilities were vastly decreased in comparison to my recent overseas position." Another commented, "I was shocked at the animosity of coworkers because I had learned to successfully work with Japanese during my international assignment!" After experiences like this, repatriates learn to "keep their mouths shut about their international expertise." By so doing, home country coworkers or supervisors can frustrate the strategic purposes of the international assignment. To avoid these potentially significant problems, you should look for opportunities to pass on general articles about cross-cultural and repatriation adjustment, as well as create opportunities to talk with coworkers and supervisors about the process.

Take Advantage of Information Sources

Several available sources of information will enable you to accurately mold expectations, including sponsors, prereturn training and orientation, home country visits, and general home-country information.

Throughout the international assignment, and especially just before the return, sponsors can provide important information to you. If you have not had a sponsor during the assignment, it is still important to try to locate one in order to make the coming-home process more effective. The information a sponsor provides will generally focus on company-related changes, but may also provide you with general information about changes in the home country. In addition, past expatriates suggest finding "family sponsors" who would stay in touch with you and your family during and after the assignment.

Training and orientations can provide essential information. You will need information about changes in company and culture, about how to interact with home country nationals (again), and about changes in the general living environment. Job-related information might focus on structural and political changes in the firm, technological innovations, procedural changes, and so on. This training might include warnings about the general lack of interest home nationals might have in your international experiences. This lack of interest may be felt at work and after work. Finally, take advantage of training and orientation that include information about housing situations, financial compensation changes, tax laws, school systems, price levels, and so on.

Along with training and sponsors, make visits to the home country throughout the international assignment and especially just before returning home. As mentioned, two-thirds of the U.S. expatriates receive paid home leave from their companies; however, only one-third of companies require their expatriates to take home leave in their home country. Avoid the very real temptation to use the home leave allowance to visit every place but home.

Plan for Housing

Locating and acquiring adequate housing is a major challenge for many repatriates and has a major impact on spouse adjustment after coming home. Some repatriates' spouses have had positive experiences: "Coming back to our own home really helped . . . we had a place to identify with friends and neighbors who cared about us. It also helped being in the same school upon return since we were in contact with teachers during the assignment and they remembered us."

If you didn't keep your home during the international assignment or if you are returning to a city different from the one you left, you will need assistance in locating, purchasing, and moving into a new home. Take advantage of any house-hunting trips offered during the last few months of your assignment. If the house-selection process must occur after your return, take advantage of any time allowed in locating a new house.

Seek Out Expatriate and Spouse Support Groups

Repatriates and spouses often suggested that firms consider providing informal opportunities to meet and socialize with other repatriates and their families. This would provide them the opportunity to share international experiences, and as one spouse said, "Support groups could help us answer the many questions a returning family has. A great many changes occur during the international assignment, and searching for the answers alone can be most frustrating and cause needless tension in the family unit." For a firm, this is a relatively costless endeavor that may provide important benefits to those involved. However, few firms provide this assistance, and so you will probably need to initiate efforts in this regard. Most experienced international managers are happy to share their experiences and advice, so don't be shy about seeking out experienced employees.

Plan for "Down Time"

The challenges of coming home to a new work and home routine will require a significant amount of your time. Experienced expatriates recommended taking two weeks off to get settled in. Some even thought firms should "force" repatriates to take time off. Regardless of the amount of time, the important thing is that firms allow some period of time to make the transition after you return home.

CONCLUSION

Hopefully, at this point you are both nervous and excited about your return home. If you are nervous, we hope it is because you realize that repatriation is filled with challenges. If you are excited, we hope it is because you recognize that repatriation is rich in opportunities. No doubt there are human resource managers, line executives, and experienced international managers who want your return to be a successful one. Leverage their good intentions and knowledge. However, nothing can compensate for your own thorough understanding of the repatriation process and the factors that affect it, and then taking steps to ensure your own and your family's success. The following summarizes the key steps you can take to ensure that, like the space shuttle, your reentry is a spectacular success.

KEYS TO SUCCESSFUL REPATRIATION

- Begin with the end in mind.

- Plan early for your return.

- Keep your expectations realistic.

- Expect repatriation-adjustment difficulties.

- Assess the likely difficulty of your reentry.

- Define the strategic function of your repatriation.

- Select a repatriation team.

- Find a sponsor.

- Look for a suitable job with some autonomy.

- Look for opportunity to add value versus a promotion.

- Take advantage of home leave to keep in touch.

- Take advantage of repatriation training offered.

- Ask about the repatriation process and policies.

- Spend extra time understanding your company's housing policies related to repatriation.

- Thoroughly investigate housing conditions and prices before your return.

- Seek out experienced international managers for sources of individual and family support.

- Discuss needed financial adjustments in advance.

- Prepare a repatriation budget.

- Mentally prepare for not being quite so special.

- Take some down time.

- Take advantage of any job-finding assistance for spouses offered.

INDEX